MW00986818

GRINNING WITH
THE GIPPER

GRINNING WITH THE GIPPER

A Celebration of the Wit, Wisdom, and Wisecracks of Ronald Reagan

Edited by James S. Denton
with Peter Schweizer

A MORGAN ENTREKIN BOOK
THE ATLANTIC MONTHLY PRESS
NEW YORK

◆

Copyright © 1988 by James S. Denton and Peter Schweizer

All rights reserved. No part of this book may be reproduced in any form or by
any electronic or mechanical means including information storage and retrieval
systems without permission in writing from the publisher, except by a reviewer,
who may quote brief passages in a review.

Published simultaneously in Canada
Printed in the United States of America

Library of Congress Cataloging-in-Publication Data

Reagan, Ronald.
    Grinning with the Gipper : the wit, wisdom, and wisecracks of
Ronald Reagan / edited by James S. Denton with Peter Schweizer.
    "A Morgan Entrekin book."
    ISBN 0-87113-272-9
    1. Reagan, Ronald—Quotations. 2. Reagan, Ronald—Humor.
3. United States—Politics and government—1981- —Humor.
I. Denton, James S. II. Schweizer, Peter, 1964- . III. Title.
E838.5.R432 1988   88-17552   973.927'092'4—dc19 .

The Atlantic Monthly Press
19 Union Square West
New York, NY 10003

FIRST PRINTING

Contents

"Somehow you knew that I'd
get around to a story, didn't you?"
—Ronald Reagan

*To Ronald Reagan,
whose faith in America
has restored our own*

Preface

I was first struck by Ronald Reagan's masterful use of humor while attending a briefing on tax reform at the White House at which the President spoke several months into his second term. He was on a roll: "There are some in government who have a very simple tax proposal in mind. There will be only two lines on the tax form: How much did you make last year? Send it."

Then, a couple of months later, at a similar occasion, there he was again warming up his audience with a fresh comedy routine which made him impossible not to like. But what is more, somehow this President of the United States was making each person out there feel that he liked them. Personally.

All in a day's work for the Great Communicator.

But it occurred to me that beyond their entertainment value, these witticisms illuminated something about Ronald Reagan's persona and his enormous popularity which has so bewildered the all-knowing political pols. It has to do with this President's unmodern view of the world and of his role in it.

I remember a particularly telling Reagan remark following a just-a-bit-too-long introduction by the late Claire Booth Luce. In her introduction, Mrs. Luce, who had her own sense of high drama, recalled some tortured passages from the memoirs of former Presidents which droned on stoically to the heavy burdens, the personal sacrifice, and the endless suffering endured by history's Lonely Titans of the Oval Office.

When she finished, the President stood with that trademark gee-whiz expression on his face, cocked his head as he does, and said something like, "Well . . . Claire, I must be doing something wrong. I'm kind of enjoying myself."

And everyone in that room knew he meant it.

This book tells that story and paints a self-portrait of a human being—perhaps the world's most important one—not oblivious but undaunted, unintimidated yet refreshingly unpretentious. A man supremely comfortable with himself.

These days that's uncommon, and in politics it is a downright rarity. And therein lies the key to Ronald Reagan's success. And that's why this book was assembled. You see no one told the President that his was a miserable job and it certainly hadn't occurred to him. No torment, no hang-ups—let's just set our sights, be civil, and do our damn best.

That's what it is all about in this country. And we all know it and that's why we'll miss Ronald Reagan.

Besides Ronald Reagan, there is a handful of friends without whose help this little project never would have made it. Peter Schweizer's late nights with his word processor and his constant badgering of me to move along were indispensable. Plus, although it was more fun than

work, Peter was a big help on the creative side organizing
the presentation. P. J. O'Rourke, who is Ronald Reagan's
only living rival in the commonsense humorist category,
gave the book an enormous boost with his contribution.
Finally many thanks to Morgan Entrekin, and his associate
Anton Mueller, for taking a chance with this slightly out-
of-character book for the Atlantic Monthly Press.

JAMES S. DENTON
Washington, D.C.

Introduction

by P.J. O'Rourke

Ronald Reagan has endured more scrutiny in office than any American President. Not much of this nosing around has been friendly. And some of the intrusions upon our Chief Executive's person have been personal indeed. While recovering from colon surgery, the President himself said, "As if the independent counsel, a special review board, and two congressional committees weren't enough, there was my trip to Bethesda. I tell you, one more probe and I've had it."

The problem is, we've been looking at the wrong end of this President. What's interesting about Ronald Reagan is neither his polyps nor his political appointees but his mind. Of course puling Democrats and zealots of international Goody-Two-Shoe-ism will say the President doesn't have a mind and doesn't mind if he doesn't. But that can't be true. Ronald Reagan has been elected twice, almost by acclaim, to the highest office in the land. He has mothered prosperity, murdered inflation in its bed, and saved America from becoming a giant roll of geopolitical bathroom tissue. He's given the Russians a taste of their own guerrilla RX in Afghanistan, Angola, and Nicaragua and forced that wishy-washy liberal, Gorbachev, to come to heel at the arms control bargaining table. And Ronald Reagan has galvanized his nation without once resorting to FDR bullyrag or JFK eyewash. The man must have something topside.

What that something is will be obvious to the reader of this collection: President Reagan has a sense of humor. It's not just that he's funny. We've had plenty of funny Presidents lately. Some looked funny. Most acted funny. And there was definitely something funny going on with one or two of them. But President Reagan can make a joke as well as be one. And the jokes he's made show a sense of humor as that phrase should be defined. Ronald Reagan has a sense of proportion, a sense of how life is and always will be. "There's a difficult thing about cutting expenses— the expenses can vote," said the President as he handed a check for a highway project to New York's hopeless Mayor Koch.

President Reagan understands the "humors," the ruling passions, that beset men and institutions. Discussing the rebates sent to taxpayers while he was governor of California, Reagan said, "I remember the third time we did that, a long-time senator, state senator, came into my office one day outraged about our giving that money back to the people. And he said that he considered giving that money back to the people an unnecessary expenditure of public funds."

And, as with all great humorists, Ronald Reagan can go to the heart of a matter with precision and brevity that shame drab think-tankers and ponderous weenies at *The New York Review of Books*:

. . . government's view of the economy could be
summed up in a few short phrases: If it moves, tax it.
If it keeps moving, regulate it. And if it stops moving,
subsidize it.

A picture of Ronald Reagan drawn from his humor
shows a man we undervalue, however well we like him. Try
collecting the jokes of Walter Mondale, George Bush, or
Michael Dukakis. Try, especially, collecting the jokes they
tell about themselves. "I've been getting some flak for
ordering the production of the B-1," Reagan said at the
USO's fortieth anniversary dinner. "How did I know it was
an airplane? I thought it was vitamins for the troops."
"There are advantages to being elected President," he told
the graduating class at Glassboro High School. "The day
after I was elected, I had my high school grades classified
Top Secret."

Not many American Presidents have been confident
enough to be humble. Only Lincoln and Coolidge were as
self-effacing as Reagan. And even they might not have had
the guts to say:

For me politics is forgive and, as you may have heard,
sometimes forget.

I've laid down the law, though, to everyone from now
on about anything that happens, that no matter what
time it is, wake me, even if it's in the middle of a
Cabinet meeting.

This courage didn't fail President Reagan on March
30, 1981, when an addled movie buff (a Jodie Foster fan, of
all things) tried to assassinate him. "If I had this much
attention in Hollywood, I'd have stayed there," he told the

panicked staff in the emergency room. "Please tell me you're Republicans," he said to the surgical team. And to an attentive nurse: "Does Nancy know about us?"

The President not only kept his cool under fire, he kept his perspective. When Lyn Nofziger rushed in to tell his wounded boss that everything in Washington was "running normally," Reagan replied, "What makes you think I'd be happy about that?"

Victims of liberal hyperactivity may say that our President is *too* phlegmatic under pressure. They would claim he's in intellectual hibernation. But he's wide awake enough to goose his critics:

> There are some things that are current today and sweeping the country that I haven't had time to get familiar with—Pac Man, for example. . . . I asked about it and somebody told me that it was a round thing that gobbled up money. I thought that was Tip O'Neill.

Time and again Ronald Reagan has proved himself faster on the draw than the pundits gunning for him.

> Sam Donaldson: What about Mondale's charges?
> The President: He ought to pay them.

> Question: What are you going to tell the Chinese ambassador?
> The President: Hello.

Ready wit makes Ronald Reagan a tough opponent. And wit that tells the truth is hard to parry. Nobody knows this better, by now, than the Soviets. President Reagan has loosed a more frightening weapon than SDI on communism; he's made it the free world's laughingstock.

Did you hear that the Communists now have a million-dollar lottery for their people? The winners get a dollar a year for a million years.

And George Shultz brought me back one from the Soviet Union the other day. It seems they went in to the General Secretary and told him there was an elderly lady there in the Kremlin who wouldn't leave without seeing him. And he said, "Well, bring her in." And they did. And he said, "Old Mother, what is it? What can I do?" She says, "I have one question." She said, "Was communism invented by a politician or a scientist?" And he said, "Well, a politician." She said, "That explains it. A scientist would have tried it on mice first."

The humor in this book is the humor of a man who knows what he believes in with a certainty that precludes fanaticism. It is also the humor of a man who is able to believe in himself without drowning in the slime of megalomania.

They tell me I'm the most powerful man in the world. I don't believe that. Over there in that White House someplace there's a fellow that puts a piece of paper on my desk every day that tells me what I'm going to be doing every fifteen minutes. He's the most powerful man in the world.

The jokes, quips, and funny stories gathered here come from from a person who's temperate, decent, stouthearted, smart, resilient, and reasonable—but not perfect. The Reagan presidency has had its errors and omissions. Ronald Reagan would be the first to admit that and the last to make excuses for it.

> . . . if we mean to continue governing [we] must realize that it will not always be so easy to place the blame on the past for our national difficulties. You know, one day the great baseball manager Frankie Frisch sent a rookie out to play center field. The rookie promptly dropped the first fly ball that was hit to him. On the next play he let a grounder go between his feet and then threw the ball to the wrong base. Frankie stormed out of the dugout, took his glove away from him, and said, "I'll show you how to play this position." And the next batter slammed a line drive right over second base. Frankie came in on it, missed it completely, fell down when he tried to chase it, threw down his glove, and yelled at the rookie, "You've got center field so screwed up nobody can play it."

We're going to miss this President. And when, in the midst of carping political debates, we are blaming him for this or castigating him for that, we should think back to what this country was like eight years ago. We were in the slough of emotional and financial despond. We were a glum and diminished nation afflicted with a leadership that was philosophically and politically dead, but too dumb to lie down. America is a happier, richer, better place now. Funnier, too. We're grinning again. And we owe a lot of that to President Reagan. We can laugh with him. We can laugh at him—he won't mind. But let's not treat the President the way the preacher treated the farmer in one more of Ronald Reagan's jokes:

> . . . the old farmer . . . took over a parcel of land down near the creek bottom. It had never been cleared, it was covered with rocks, brush, all rutted,

and he just determined to make it flourish. And he went to work and he hauled away the rocks and fertilized and so forth, and then planted his garden. . . .

And he was so proud of what he'd accomplished that one Sunday after church he asked the minister to drop by and see his place. Well, the reverend came out and he was impressed. He said, "That's the tallest corn I've ever seen. The Lord certainly has blessed this land." And then he said, "Those melons! I've never seen any bigger than that. Praise the Lord." And he went on that way—tomatoes, squash, the beans, everything, and what the Lord had done with that land. And the old farmer . . . finally he couldn't take it anymore and he said, "Reverend, I wish you could have seen it when the Lord was doing it by Himself."

GRINNING WITH THE GIPPER

Ronald Reagan
on the Gipper

"It's true hard work never killed anybody, but I figure why take the chance."
—*To the annual Gridiron Dinner; 4/22/87*

"I've been getting some flak about ordering the production of the B-1. How did I know it was an airplane? I thought it was vitamins for the troops."
—*Remarks at a dinner marking the fortieth anniversary of the U.S.O.; 10/17/81*

"These last few weeks have really been hectic what with Libya, Nicaragua, and the budget and taxes. I don't know about you, but I've been working long hours. I've really been burning the midday oil."
—*Remarks at the White House Correspondents' Association dinner; 4/17/86*

[After the U.S. Navy shot down two Libyan jets over the Gulf of Sidra]
"And there's been a lot of talk, and the press has been very concerned, because six hours went by before they awoke

1

me at 4:30 in the morning to tell me about it. And there's a very good answer to that. Why? If our planes were shot down, yes, they'd wake me up right away; if the other fellow's were shot down, why wake me up?"
   —*Remarks and a question-and-answer session with Orange County Republicans in Costa Mesa, Calif.; 8/20/81*

[After reports that the President took long naps]
"Well, I hope that you'll find your day here a useful and productive one, and I hope you will also relax and enjoy yourselves. Don't relax too much—as you know, my staff is rather reluctant about waking people up."
   —*Remarks and a question-and-answer session with a group of out-of-town editors; 10/5/81*

"Well, I know this: I've laid down the law, though, to everyone from now on about anything that happens, that no matter what time it is, wake me, even if it's in the middle of a Cabinet meeting."
   —*Remarks at the annual dinner of the White House Correspondents' Association; 4/13/84*

"You know, this has been a wonderful time. Oh, I had a little difficulty with a knife and fork. Nancy wasn't here to help me cut my meat."
   —*Remarks at the annual Senate-House fund-raising dinner; 5/10/84*

[To members of the press]
"We're all Americans together and we believe in the same ideals. It's good to be here and for you folks on the beat tomorrow, sleep late. I'm going to."
   —*To the annual Gridiron Dinner; 4/23/85*

"In the last month, there was a radio address to the nation on Labor Day, a TV address on the economy, a new conference that covered the waterfront of issues. I've had an opportunity to do some traveling, to talk to union members in Chicago about the housing industry, to help get Westway started in New York City, assist at the dedication of President Ford's museum in Grand Rapids, Michigan, and talk to the Republican women leaders in Denver about Wall Street and Main Street. Last week in New Orleans, I announced some major initiatives on crime and also spoke to the World Bank conference about our new development policy. And when I leave you I'm going to be speaking to the National Alliance of Business about mobilizing the private sector to assist the underprivileged. Now, during all of this, we've had the usual round of White House activities, ranging from a luncheon for black college leaders to some very fruitful diplomatic discussions, including a visit from Prime Minister Begin in Israel. Now, I think that's pretty good for a fellow that only works two or three hours a day."
—*Remarks and a question-and-answer session with a group of out-of-town editors; 10/5/81*

James McCartney, president of the Gridiron Dinner: "I've seen it reported that you're just a president of image and no substance. But I understand that you often take home serious reports and documents to read at night. And I'm told that you often pick up one of those serious reports or documents to study—during the commercials."
The President: "You made a slight mistake. I read the papers while the news is on. I watch the commercials."
—*To the annual Gridiron Dinner; 4/22/87*

"But there are advantages to being elected President. The day after I was elected, I had my high school grades classified Top Secret."
> —*Remarks to the graduating class of Glassboro High School, N.J.; 6/19/86*

"I confess, I was not as attentive as I might have been during my classroom days. I seem to remember my parents being told, 'Young Ron is trying—very trying.' "
> —*Remarks at the annual convention of the National Parent-Teacher Association in Albuquerque, N.M.; 6/15/83*

"You know, I was devoted to some other activities, such as football and swimming and campus dramatics. And I've often wondered since, if I'd spent more time and worked harder as a student how far I might have gone."
> —*Remarks at the Uniformed Services university commencement ceremony; 5/16/87*

"I'll tell you another bad thing about my youth. When I was playing football, the cheerleaders were boys."
> —*Remarks to students at Hickman High School, Columbia, Mo.; 3/26/87*

[To the interpreter during an interview with the French newspaper *Le Figaro*]
"You know, your having to interpret for me is something of a reflection on my early education, because when I was a schoolboy, I studied French for a couple of years. And then, 1949—the first time I ever set foot in your country—I found myself with a couple, a married couple. The three of us were driving down across France to the Mediterranean.

And I discovered that even though they were English and just twenty miles away, they had never been to France. They did not know one word of French. And I was going to be the only thing between us and silence. We were coming to a town for lunch. And I started to remember—that was a long time ago—so I could remember some of what I'd learned in my French study. So we came to the town, and I mentally figured how I'm going to find lunch. So, it was 'gendarme.' And I rolled down the window of the car, and I said: 'Pardon, monsieur, j'ai grand faim. Où est le meilleur café?' And he told me where was the best café. And the friend that was driving says: 'What did he say?' And I said, 'I haven't the slightest idea. I memorized the questions, never the answers.'"
—*12/22/83*

"History's no easy subject. Even in my day it wasn't, and we had so much less of it to learn then."
—*Remarks to the winners of the Bicentennial of the Constitution National Essay Contest; 9/10/87*

"I was the drum major, and my older brother—he played the bass horn. And I had an incident when we were in a neighboring town on Decoration Day—we were leading the parade. And the marshal of the parade, on his horse, had ridden back to see how everything was coming. And he didn't get back quite up to the head of the parade in time. And there I was, waving that baton. I knew that the music was sounding further and further away. He had come in time to turn the band but not me. And I was walking down the street all by myself, and the band had turned the corner."
—*Remarks to participants in the National YMCA Youth Governor's Conference; 6/21/84*

"When I was attending college—now, I know many of you probably think that was back when there were dinosaurs roaming the Earth—actually, they weren't; it was about the time when Moses was parting the Red Sea."
    —Remarks at the Tuskegee University commence-
    ment ceremony; 5/10/87

"And you know, not too long ago I was questioned about the George Gipp story. And this interviewer had really done his research. In fact he'd even gone back and talked to my old football coach, Ralph McKenzie, at Eureka College, who was ninety-one years old, and asked him about my football career. Well, now, I've been through a lot of interviews, but believe me, I tensed up at hearing that. And apparently Mac described me as 'eager, aggressive, better on defense, overall an average football player—but an outstanding talker.' "
    —Remarks at Notre Dame University, South Bend,
    Ind.; 3/9/88

"But one thing I'll always cherish about Eureka [College] besides lessons in football and humility is that the college took a chance on me. Now, my family couldn't pay for the schooling. We didn't live on the wrong side of the tracks, but we lived close enough that we could hear the whistles."
    —Remarks at a scholarship fund-raising dinner, Eu-
    reka College, Eureka, Ill.; 9/23/86

"People ask me if I'm looking at my college years, if I can remember any inkling that I would someday run for President. Well, actually, the thought first struck me on graduation day, when the president of the college handed me my

diploma and asked, 'Are you better off today than you were four years ago?' "
  —*Remarks at Eureka College in Eureka, Ill.; 2/6/84*

"Some years after I graduated from Eureka College, I returned to that school. And they gave me an honorary degree, which only compounded a sense I'd nursed for twenty-five years, because I thought the first one they gave me was honorary."
  —*Remarks on receiving the final report of the National Commission on Excellence in Education; 4/26/83*

"It was a teacher who steered me into acting, an English teacher named B. J. Fraser, back in Dixon, Illinois. He's gone now, but I somehow can imagine him saying, 'But I take no responsibility for his going into politics.' "
  —*Remarks at a White House ceremony honoring the National Teacher of the Year; 4/9/84*

"And from there I went to Hollywood, because the other great interest that I'd had besides going to classes in the college was in student theatricals, acting in plays and dramas. So I wound up in Hollywood. And I have to say that today, not only the economics and the athletics still serve me in good stead in the job I'm in. You'd be surprised how much being a good actor pays off."
  —*Remarks and a question-and-answer session with students at Fudan University in Shanghai, China; 4/30/84*

[To educators in Whittier, Calif.]
"And the only reason that I'm leaving here is because I
have a date, and I don't want to keep them waiting with one
of their summer classes in remedial reading. And I want to
go out and join them. They probably invited me because
they've heard some of my old speeches."
                                               —6/30/83

"Some years ago, when I was just beginning in Hollywood
in the motion picture business, I had been sentenced for
the few years I'd been there to movies that the studio didn't
want good, it wanted them Thursday."
        —Remarks in New York at the eighty-fourth annual
          dinner of the Irish American Historical Society;
          11/6/81

[Toasting President Anwar Sadat of Egypt]
"Now Mr. President, I know that you struggled many
years and played a prominent role in creating an organiza-
tion which brought independence to your country. But
then on the night of the revolution, when it actually began,
you were in a movie theater watching a picture with your
family. Now, you wouldn't by chance remember who happened to be in that movie, would you? I never won an
Oscar, but a revolution would do."
                                               —8/5/81

"Thank you for that warm greeting and that applause, and
since that applause is coming from veterans, I have to ask:
Is it for how I'm doing in my job, or how I'm doing on the
Late Late Show in *Hellcats of the Navy*?"
        —Remarks at the annual convention of the veterans of
        Foreign Wars in New Orleans, La.; 8/15/83

[Remarks to the world champion Kansas City Royals]
"I pitched in a World Series, but I was with the Cardinals at the time. Three games—it was the 1926 World Series, but I was doing it in a 1952 movie."
      —*10/31/85*

"Although I'm an old horse cavalryman myself, I've always had a soft spot in my heart for the Navy. Back in my former profession, I played a naval officer in *Hellcats of the Navy*. And Nancy was a Navy nurse in the same picture. Now, speaking for myself only, if they should send me another script, it probably would be for *Old Man and the Sea*."
      —*Address at commencement exercises for the United States Naval Academy; 5/22/85*

"In those days American motion pictures occupied more than seventy-five percent of the playing time of all the screens in the world. Unfortunately the movies that we sent overseas sometimes—well, they weren't always successful. I had one called *Cattle Queen of Montana*. It lost something in Japanese."
      —*Remarks on signing World Trade Week proclamation; 5/19/86*

[After touring the American cowboy exhibit at the Library of Congress]
"Thank you very much. We have just had a tour of the exhibit, and as we went along I kept looking and looking for something from *Cattle Queen of Montana*. I wasn't the cattle queen—Barbara Stanwyck was."
      —*3/24/83*

[To members of the Country Music Association during a
television performance]
"I had to bring my own cue cards."
    —*3/16/83*

"A sunny spring day, I was walking down Fifth Avenue,
New York. And from about thirty feet away, a man says,
'Ah, I know you. I see you all the—' Well, he went on with
all of that, and he started stalking me, coming toward me.
Everyone else fell back and kind of just stood watching.
And he's fumbling in his pocket all the time. He gets to me,
shoves a piece of paper and a pen out at me for an auto-
graph and says, 'Ray Milland.' So I signed Ray Milland."
    —*Remarks at the tenth anniversary dinner of the Eth-
        ics and Public Policy Center, Washington, D.C.;
        11/18/86*

"By the way, I've been asked at times what it is like to sit
and watch the Late Late Show and see yourself; and I have
one answer. It's like looking at a son you never knew you
had."
    —*Remarks at a White House briefing for representa-
        tives of service organizations; 7/30/86*

[After being presented with a bushel of tomatoes]
"In the business I used to be in, you worried about them
throwing these at you."
    —*Remarks to the New Jersey Republican State Com-
        mittee; 10/13/87*

[After being presented with an award that resembles the Motion Picture Academy's Oscar]
"And I wasn't acting at all. But then there were some who said that I wasn't before."

> —*Remarks at a White House ceremony marking the beginning of the Summer Youth Employment Program; 5/7/84*

"While I was governor of California, I was asked on several occasions to represent the United States at functions across the border in Mexico. And at one of these at which I spoke to a rather large audience, I made my speech, and then I sat down to rather unenthusiastic and scattered applause. And I was a little embarrassed. In fact, I was very self-conscious. I thought maybe I'd said something wrong. I was doubly embarrassed when the next speaker got up and, speaking' in Spanish, which I didn't understand; he was getting enthusiastic applause almost every other line. Well, to hide my embarrassment, I decided that I'd start clapping before anyone else, and I'd clap louder and longer than anyone else. And a few minutes of that, and our ambassador leaned over to me and said, 'I wouldn't do that if I were you. He's interpreting your speech.'"

> —*Remarks at Cinco de Mayo ceremonies in San Antonio, Tex.; 5/5/83*

"And I remember that I was up at that great installation in the state of Washington where so much was being done with nuclear power. And in one particular building where they were showing me through, why, we put on felt boots and we put on some gowns and then we went through. But then we had to peel all of this off. And there was a slot

machine there in which you put your hands and your feet—
and there were four dials that started ticking away as to the
amount of radioactivity that you might have acquired in
your extremities. And mine all—on all three of them,
stopped. But on my left hand, that dial kept on ticking, and
it was getting up there toward the numbers that were red.
And I was getting a little concerned. And the manager of
the plant looked over my shoulder, and he says, 'Oh, your
left hand.' He says, 'That always happens. That's the radium dial on your wristwatch.' I was very relieved.

I was two hundred miles away from there when I
realized—I don't have a radium dial. Every once in a while,
I still put my head under the covers and look to see if my
hand is lighting up."
—Remarks at the presentation ceremony for the En-
rico Fermi awards at the Department of Energy;
4/25/83

[After receiving a Thanksgiving turkey from the National
Turkey Federation]
"This, of course, is a great tradition of Thanksgiving in our
country, and I'm very happy—we used to do this all the
time in California, with the association. And they came to
the office, and I had a few adventures there, too. Finally
one day they turned to a custom of actually bringing it
cooked, and we would have a lunch right there with the
staff in the office. But I had to carve it for all those
gentlemen and ladies of the press with their cameras on
me. And I remember one day I was carving, and I thought
they hadn't cooked it very well, because there was a lot of
blood appearing, which didn't look very appetizing. I
found out I'd cut my thumb."
—11/18/81

"And I was on my way to work one morning with the car radio on, and I heard a disc jockey. And out of the clear blue sky he spoke a line that endeared him to me forever. He said, 'Every man should take unto himself a wife, because sooner or later something is bound to happen that you can't blame on the governor.'"

> —*Remarks at a state Republican fund-raising luncheon in Parsippany, N.J.; 10/11/85*

"What I remember most is discovering that after spending a whole [presidential] campaign talking about the serious problems we faced, I got into office and found out I'd been guilty of understatement. I felt a little like the *Titanic* passenger John Jacob Astor, who it is reported said when the ship hit the iceberg, 'Listen, I asked for ice but this is ridiculous.'"

> —*Remarks at a White House briefing on the Criminal Justice Reform Act of 1987; 10/16/87*

[Referring to the assassination attempt when Secret Service agents pushed the President into his limousine]
"If I could give you just one little bit of advice, when somebody tells you to get in a car quick, do it."

> —*Remarks by telephone at the annual dinner of the White House Correspondents' Association; 4/25/81*

[To the hospital staff upon entering the hospital, referring to John Hinckley]
"Does anybody know what that guy's beef was?"

> —*3/30/81*

[To surgeons as he entered the operating room]
"Please tell me you're Republicans."

> —*3/30/81*

[To Nancy, after she first arrived at the hospital]
"Honey, I forgot to duck."
       —3/30/81

[To daughter Maureen by telephone, shortly after the operation]
"The bullet ruined one of my best suits."
       —3/30/81

[Paraphrasing Winston Churchill]
"There's no more exhilarating feeling than being shot at without result."
       —3/30/81

[To an attentive nurse, during recovery]
"Does Nancy know about us?"
       —4/1/81

[After being surrounded by an attentive medical staff]
"If I had this much attention in Hollywood, I'd have stayed there."
       —3/30/81

"I have a letter with me. The letter came from Peter Sweeney. He's in the second grade in the Riverside School in Rockville Centre, and he said, 'I hope you get well quick or you might have to make a speech in your pajamas.' He added a postscript. 'P.S. If you have to make a speech in your pajamas, I warned you.'"
       —Address before a joint session of the Congress on
       the Program for Economic Recovery; 4/28/81

[After spending time in Bethesda Medical Center for an operation]
"This is the first time that I've been with many of you since spending a little time in Bethesda, and Nancy and I want you to know how much your prayers and well-wishes and good wishes meant to us. We sat together and read many of the get-well cards that you sent. Knowing you were with us in spirit was the best medicine of all. Some of those cards were pretty special and pretty memorable. Just one in particular said, 'Dear Mr. President, I was very concerned to hear that the doctors took two feet out of your inner workings. How did those two feet get in there?'"

> *Remarks at a Texas state Republican Party fund-raising dinner; 8/22/85*

[After recuperating from colon surgery at Bethesda Medical Center while the Iran-Contra investigation was under way]
"As if the independent counsel, a special review board, and two congressional committees weren't bad enough, there was my trip to Bethesda. I tell you, one more probe and I've had it."

> *—Annual Gridiron Dinner; 4/28/87*

"With the Iran [Contra] thing occupying everyone's attention, I was thinking: Do you remember the flap when I said, 'We begin bombing in five minutes?' Remember when I fell asleep during my audience with the pope? Remember Bitburg? . . . Boy, those were the good old days."

> *—Annual Gridiron Dinner, 4/28/87*

"I've been looking forward to meeting with you today, welcoming you here to the White House. You know, around the turn of the century there was an English gentleman, Samuel Butler, who remarked that the advantage of doing one's praising of one's self is that I can lay it on so thick in exactly the right places."

—*Remarks on the Program for Economic Recovery at a White House reception for business and government leaders; 6/11/81*

"I was just in Venice. They must have had a hard spring, because from the helicopter when I looked down, all the streets seemed to be flooded."

—*Remarks to the People-to-People High School Student Ambassadors program; 7/24/87*

"Nancy and the President [of France] started toward their table in the dining room with everyone standing around their tables waiting for us. Mrs. Mitterand [the French President's wife] and I started through the tables, the butler leading us through the people. And suddenly Mrs. Mitterand stopped and she calmly turned her head and said something to me in French, which, unfortunately, I did not understand. And the butler was motioning for us to come on, and I motioned to her that we should go forward, that we were to get to the other side of the room. And, again, very calmly, she made her statement to me. And then the interpreter caught up with us. She was telling me that I was standing on her gown."

—*Remarks at the National Leadership Forum of the Center of International and Strategic Studies of Georgetown University; 4/6/84*

"Jesse Helms wants me to move to the right; Lowell Weicker wants me to move to the left; Teddy Kennedy wants me to move back to California."
    —*Remarks at the annual Salute to Congress dinner; 2/4/81*

"Now, this is the first time that I've really been out on the stump since I was in the hospital, and I missed doing this. I missed it. I even miss hecklers."
    —*Remarks at the Santa-Cali-Gon-Days celebration in Independence, Mo.; 9/2/85*

[To a crowd of administration supporters at the Conservative Political Action Conference]
"And in the rough days ahead, and I know there will be such days, I hope that you'll be like the mother of the young lad in camp when the camp director told her that he was going to have to discipline her son. And she said, 'Well, don't be too hard on him. He's very sensitive. Slap the boy next to him, and that will scare Irving.'"
    —*3/20/81*

"You know, these last several weeks, I've felt a little bit like that farmer that was driving his horse and wagon to town for some grain and had a head-on collision with a truck. And later there was the litigation involving claims for his injuries—some of them permanent. And he was on the stand and a lawyer said to him, 'Isn't it true that while you were lying there at the scene of the accident and you said you never felt better in your life?' And he said, 'Yes, I remember that.' Well, later he's on the stand and the witnesses were there—the lawyer for the other side is questioning and he said, 'When you gave that answer about

how you felt, what were the circumstances?' 'Well,' he
said, 'I was lying there and a car came up and a deputy
sheriff got out.' He said, 'My horse was screaming with
pain—had broken two legs. The deputy took out his gun,
put it in the horse's ear, and finished him off. And,' he said,
'my dog was whining with pain—had a broken back. And,'
he said, 'he went over to him and put the gun to his ear.
And then,' he says, 'he turned to me and says, 'Now, how
are you feeling?' "

> —*Remarks by the President at the Conservative Polit-
> ical Action Committee luncheon; 2/20/87*

[After repeated chants of "Four more years" from the
audience]
"Thank you very much. And since the Constitution has
something to say about what you've just been chanting, I'll
assume that you're suggesting that I live four more years."

> —*Remarks at a rally for Senator Mark Andrews in
> Grand Forks, N.D.; 10/17/86*

Question: Will you be happy if you get some of what you
want, but not all?"
The President: "Oh, ninety-seven percent I could live
with."

> —*Exchange with reporters on the Program for Eco-
> nomic Recovery; 2/19/81*

Question: "What are you going to tell the Chinese ambassador?"
The President: "Hello."

> —*Informal exchange with reporters; 4/7/83*

Question: "How is your hearing?"
The President: "What?"
   —*Informal exchange with reporters in Los Angeles, Calif.; 8/22/83*

[After Mikhail Gorbachev appeared on the cover of *Time* magazine wearing a pin-striped suit]
"I'm going to do my part—after *Time* magazine, I'm going to wear my pin-striped suit to Geneva."
   —*Remarks to Republican officials; 10/7/85*

"I know all of you folks are looking forward to hearing Dick Cavett this evening. Dick feels that he was hampered on commercial television because of his image as an intellectual. I had the same problem."
   —*Remarks at the White House Correspondents' Dinner; 4/17/86*

"Now, I must say, my remarks on this occasion have not drawn rave reviews from the Soviet press. In fact, *Pravda* suggested that my remarks were hysterical and the work of an intellectual pygmy. And a Polish newspaper under the martial law there called it a cesspool of invectives, insults, and insinuation. Well, now, naturally, as a former actor, I'm somewhat sensitive about press notices like that."
   —*Remarks at the centennial meeting of the Supreme Council of the Knights of Columbus in Hartford, Conn.; 8/3/82*

"But I am aware of my age. When I go in for a physical now they no longer ask me how old I am, they just carbon date me."
   —*The annual Gridiron Dinner; 4/28/87*

[Remarks at a rally in Tampa, Fl.]
"Well, the history books tell us that one of the first visitors
to Tampa was Ponce de León. He was looking for the
Fountain of Youth. And, no, it's not true that I was with
him. If I had been, I'd have seen that he found it."
   —*10/24/86*

"I heard one presidential candidate say that what this
country needed was a president for the nineties. I was set
to run again. I thought he said a president in his nineties."
   —*The annual Gridiron Dinner; 4/28/87*

"But it's great to be with the Legion once again. You're
always so kind in your reception. But I want you to know
that the trappings of office haven't gone to my head—I still
wear the same size American Legion hat you gave me in
1980. In fact, I made the same point to Interior Secretary
Don Hodel the other day. I said, 'Don, you can't let high
office go to your head. And speaking of heads, how much
room is there left on Mount Rushmore?'"
   —*Remarks to the American Legion; 2/29/88*

"I've already lived about twenty-odd years longer than my
life expectancy when I was born. That's a source of an-
noyance to a number of people."
   —*Remarks at the Reagan administration executive
   forum; 1/20/84*

"Well, you know, the Democrats have taken special note of
every candle I add to my birthday cake. They keep hoping
that I won't be able to blow them all out. Because, you
know, your wish comes true then; and they know what I'm
wishing for."
   —*Remarks at an executive forum; 2/6/86*

"For me, politics is forgive and, as you may have heard, sometimes forget."
—*Remarks to the American Association of Editorial Cartoonists; 5/7/87*

"And I have what every man who has that many candles on his birthday cake needs around him—a large group of friends and a working sprinkler system."
—*Remarks at Eureka College in Eureka, Ill.; 2/6/84*

"My birthday cake's beginning to look more and more like a bonfire every year."
—*Remarks by the President at the Conservative Political Action Committee luncheon; 2/20/87*

"If I'm ever in need of any transplants, I got parts they don't make anymore."
—*Remarks and a question-and-answer session with regional press representatives; 2/10/86*

"In a few days I'll be celebrating another birthday which, according to some in the press, puts me on par with Moses."
—*Remarks at the annual convention of the National Religious Broadcasters; 1/31/83*

"Nancy and I are delighted to be here, and I want to thank you for the day in my life that you recognized in starting off my celebration of my thirty-first anniversary of my thirty-ninth birthday."
—*Remarks at the annual National Prayer Breakfast; 2/5/81*

"We've begun retiring our Titan ICBMs because of their old age—don't think what I'm thinking."
> —*Remarks at a White House briefing for chief executive officers of trade associations and corporations on deployment of the MX; 5/16/83*

[When asked what he felt about being seventy-two years old]
"I think that it's fine when you consider the alternatives."
> —*Remarks and a question-and-answer session with reporters on domestic and foreign policy issues; 2/4/83*

"Believe it or not, I can remember my first ride in an automobile. Most of the time it'd been horse and buggy. The horse was very fuel-efficient but kind of slow. If you want to supercharge one, you fed him an extra bag of oats."
> —*Remarks to students and faculty at Thomas Jefferson High School, Fairfax, Va.; 2/7/86*

"There's no truth to the rumor that I waved good-bye to the Donner party when they headed west."
> —*Remarks at the Santa-Cali-Gon-Days celebration in Independence, Mo.; 9/2/85*

"I've tried to start a rumor that I'm really not that old, that they mixed up the babies in the hospital."
> —*Interview with Thomas DeFrank and Eleanor Clift of* Newsweek *on the 1984 presidential election; 1/27/84*

"You will hear no criticism of age tolerated in this house. Lately, I've been heartened to remember that Moses was eighty when God commissioned him for public service, and he lived to be 120. And Abraham was 100 and his wife, Sarah, 90, when they did something truly amazing."

> —*Toast of the President to Prime Minister Menachem Begin of Israel; 9/9/81*

"I did turn seventy-five today, but remember, that's only twenty-four Celsius."

> —*Remarks at a signing ceremony for the legislative agenda and the economic report of the President; 2/6/86*

"I can define middle-aged. That's when you're faced with two temptations and you choose the one that'll get you home at nine o'clock."

> —*Remarks at the annual Salute to Congress dinner; 2/4/81*

The World's
Oldest Profession

"And just to show you how youthful I am, I intend to campaign in all thirteen states."
— *Remarks at a White House briefing for the National Alliance of Senior Citizens; 2/29/84*

[After hearing a loud bang]
"Missed me."
— *Remarks at a rally for Senator James Broyhill in Raleigh, N.C.; 10/8/86*

"Well, we've got to make certain that the American people go into the next year with their eyes open, and that's going to depend on you and Republican activists around the country. And I can't tell you how proud I am to have participated in this gathering here today and to learn that it has been as successful as it has. But let me remind you, President Dewey told me to remind you—don't get over-confident."
— *Remarks at a Nevada Republican Party fund-raising luncheon in Las Vegas, Nev.; 2/7/84*

"But it's wonderful to be here and to see so many of you from out there in the heartland of America here in Washington. I'm sure the city isn't looking its best for you, but it's just a little too chilly for the cherry blossoms yet. And most of the heated air that's normally found in Washington has moved out on the campaign trail."

> —*Remarks at an event sponsored by the American Legion Auxiliary; 3/1/84*

[After Governor Richard Lamm (D-Colo.) announced that the elderly "have a duty to die and get out of the way"]
"You guys and gals are always trying to pin me down as to which candidate worries me the most—Mondale, Hart, or Jackson. None of those. They guy that scares me is Governor Dick Lamm."

> —*Remarks at the annual dinner of the White House Correspondents' Association; 4/13/84*

[After entering the podium by walking through two lines of cheerleaders]
"You know, every once in a while, someone asks you why you campaign. Well, I just thought as I came walking down here between those two lines of lovely young ladies, why not?"

> —*Remarks at a rally for Texas Republican candidates in Irving, Tex.; 10/11/82*

"We all know that story about way back when—probably one of the first Republicans was running here in the South for office, out soliciting votes, and he was rejected by one gentleman who said to him, 'I'm a Democrat, always been a Democrat, my pappy was a Democrat, and my grandpappy was a Democrat.' And the candidate made the mistake of saying, 'Well, if your pappy was a jackass and your grandpappy was a jackass, what would that make you?' And he says, 'A Republican.' "

> *—Remarks at a fund-raising luncheon for Senator Jeremiah Denton in Burmingham, Ala.; 6/6/85*

"Now, it's no secret that this is an election year. And we've already begun to hear talk about various political strategies—the Northern strategy, the Western strategy, the Sunbelt strategy. My favorite is the Rose Garden strategy—a sure winner if all you want is the horticulture vote."

> *—Remarks at the annual Senate-House fund-raising dinner; 5/10/84*

"The other day the *Washington Post* ran a story heralding the return of spring, and I thought it was just another one of the reports on the political campaign. The headline said, 'The Sap Is Running Again.' "

> *—Remarks at the annual dinner of the White House Correspondents' Association; 4/13/84*

"Of course, the real sign of spring is our national pastime—nine guys galloping out on the field: the Democratic presidential candidates. No runs, no hits, just errors."

> *—Remarks at a Republican fund-raising dinner for congressional campaign committees; 5/12/83*

[To a large group of Republican activists in Waterloo, Iowa] "It's wonderful to see so many of you here. There are almost as many of you as there are Democratic presidential candidates."

> *—2/20/84*

"I know this isn't a partisan political affair. But I also know that you have wide-angle lenses that are wide enough to get all the Democratic presidential candidates in one shot. You just don't have a lens that's wide enough to get all their promises."

 —Remarks at the annual awards dinner of the White
 House News Photographers' Association; 5/18/83

"Is it true that young Gary Hart is having the wrinkles airbrushed in?"

 —Remarks at the annual awards dinner of the White
 House News Photographers' Association; 5/18/83

"But a lot happened while we were gone. Texaco declared bankruptcy, Senator Simon declared for the presidency, Gary Hart did both."

 —The annual Gridiron Dinner; 4/28/87

"Now, the other party had a flock of contenders, as well— so many that it gets a bit confusing at times. A few weeks ago, I read that Gephardt had announced his candidacy. I remember putting down the paper when I read that, and I said, 'Nancy, it sounds like that fellow Hartpence has changed his name again.'"

 —Remarks in Washington, D.C.; 4/29/87

"You know, I have to tell you, I love outdoor rallies like this. Once during the campaign some fellow said to me that he didn't think I was working very hard. He said, 'You've got too good a tan.' And I said, 'Well, I've been doing a lot of outdoor rallies.' And then he said, 'Well, you talk too long then.'"

 —Remarks at a Nevada Republican rally in Reno,
 Nev.; 10/17/82

Question: "Mr. President, in talking about the continuing recession tonight, you have blamed mistakes of the past, and you've blamed the Congress. Does any of the blame belong to you?"
The President: "Yes, because for many years I was a Democrat."
—*The President's news conference; 9/28/82*

"You know, the liberal tax-and-spenders keep saying: Give us another try. And that reminds me of a story of the farmer who took his son duck hunting. They were sitting there in the blind when a mallard came down, landed on the water right in front of them. Well, the father raised up his gun and fired, and the mallard just kept on sitting there peaceful as could be. He took a second shot, and when the smoke cleared, the mallard was still there, so he tried a third time. And this time the mallard took off and flew away. And the father turned to his son and said, 'Son, you have just witnessed a miracle. You've just seen a dead duck fly.' "
—*Remarks at a rally for Representative W. Henson Moore, senatorial candidate, New Orleans, La.; 9/18/86*

"In the four years before we got to Washington, they had it all. They had the whole enchilada. They controlled the presidency, the United States Senate, the House of Representatives, all the committees of Congress, and the executive branch and hundreds of agencies and departments. They virtually had a free hand, and all they could think to do with that free hand was stick it in your pocket."
—*Remarks at a Nevada Republican rally in Las Vegas, Nev.; 10/28/82*

"We need more Democrats in the Senate like Custer needed more arrows."

> —*Remarks at a fund-raising luncheon for Senator Alfonse D'Amato, in New York, N.Y.; 5/18/86*

"Now, you know, I have to say, of course, there are some things that are current today and sweeping the country that I haven't had time to get familiar with—Pac Man, for example. I don't know about him. I asked about it, and somebody told me that it was a round thing that gobbled up money. I thought that was Tip O'Neill."

> —*Remarks at a rally for Texas Republican candidates in Irving, Tex.; 10/11/82*

"And, of course, as has been made so very evident here tonight, his [Bob Hope's] other love is golf. When we met tonight, I said, 'Hello, how are you?' And he says, 'Hello, what's your handicap?' I said, 'The Congress.'"

> —*Remarks at a dinner marking the fortieth anniversary of the U.S.O.; 10/17/81*

"I know there was one young person with his parents who was up in the gallery one day at the Congress and asked who the chaplain was. And his father said, 'Well, that's the chaplain. He prays.' And his child said, 'For the Congress?' And he said, 'No; for the country.'"

> —*Remarks and a question-and-answer session with high school honors students; 5/23/83*

"Well, as I've said so often, it isn't necessary to make the Congress see the light—make them feel the heat."

> —*Remarks in Washington, D.C.; 5/24/87*

"Judi Buckalew, who recently joined my staff as a special assistant, is the first registered nurse to serve in such a capacity. Her duties aren't medical, although with what's going on in Congress, Judi, it might be a good idea if you carry smelling salts."
    —*Remarks at the annual meeting of the American Medical Association; 6/23/83*

[To the National Association of Secondary School Principals]
"When Congress leaves town, it's no accident that we call it recess."
    —*2/7/84*

"You know, we have a music hall here in Washington. It's up there on a hill; it's called the Capitol. And we've got lots of vocal talent—but we're not always so good when it comes to carrying a harmony."
    —*Remarks at the congressional barbecue; 9/18/85*

"I feel sorry for some of those Democratic Congressmen. Can you imagine what it must be like, worn out after a day at the office? They go home. They try to go to sleep. And the first thing you know, they're having nightmares that the money they're spending is their own."
    —*Remarks in Atlanta, Ga.; 1/26/84*

"And we've still got that spying problem at our embassy in Moscow. You have to use a child's magic slate to communicate. I don't know why everyone thinks that's such a big deal. The Democrats have been doing the budget on one of those for years."
    —*The annual Gridiron Dinner; 4/28/87*

"If the big spenders get their way, they'll charge everything on your taxpayer's express card and, believe me, they never leave home without it."

> —*Remarks at an Iowa caucus rally in Waterloo, Iowa; 2/29/84*

[To members of the American Retail Federation]
"I have no quarrel with the big spenders, so long as they spend their money at your stores."
> *5/16/84*

"Some politicians are kind of like the two campers who were out hiking and spotted a grizzly bear coming over the hill, and it was headed right for them. And one of them reached into his pack as quick as he could, pulled out a pair of tennis shoes, sat down, and started putting on the tennis shoes. And the other guy looked at him and said, 'You don't mean to think you can outrun a grizzly?' And the fellow with the tennis shoes stood up, and he said, 'I don't have to outrun the grizzly; I just have to outrun you.'"

> —*Remarks at a fund-raising luncheon for gubernatorial candidate Jim Bunning in Louisville, Ky.; 10/7/83*

[Referring to Senator Tim Wirth, then a Democratic candidate for the Senate in Colorado]
"He's piled up enough money to burn a wet mule."

> —*Remarks at a fund-raiser for Ken Kramer, candidate for the U.S. Senate; 9/8/86*

"Baseball, of course, is our national pastime, that is if you discount political campaigning."
—*Remarks at a White House ceremony observing National Amateur Baseball Month; 5/11/83*

[Referring to an airplane that had just taken off above him] "They're all Democrats. Run! Every time I come here they take off."
—*Remarks to participants in the Agricultural Communicators Congress; 6/25/84*

Sam Donaldson: "What about Mondale's charges?
The President: "He ought to pay them."
—*Exchange on the White House lawn, Fall 1984; from Sam Donaldson, "Oh Sam!" Washingtonian, February, 1987, p. 177*

[Speaking via satellite to Republican activists across the country]
"Good evening to all of you Republicans out there. Since I couldn't personally get to each district during the campaign this year, the RNC [Republican National Committee] came up with this marvelous means of beaming me out to gatherings all over the country. An engineer explained to me how my signal is bounced from here to a satellite and then back to all of you. I admit, I found it a little confusing. It was like listening to Walter Mondale trying to explain Teddy Kennedy."
—*10/18/82*

"I can remember when there weren't so many Republicans in California, when, not too long ago, Republicans seemed as plentiful as spring water in Death Valley. And I speak with authority, because I spent a good chunk of my life on that piece of real estate."

> —*Remarks at a California Republican Party fund-raising dinner in Long Beach, Calif.; 6/30/83*

"I had an uncle who was a Democrat in Chicago. He received a silver cup from the party for never having missed voting in fifteen elections. He'd been dead for fourteen of them."

> —*Remarks at the annual Salute to Congress dinner; 2/4/81*

"I've been spending some of my time trying to meet the Democratic members of Congress halfway, and the halfway house I found is Tip O'Neill's office."

> —*Remarks at the annual Salute to Congress dinner; 2/4/81*

[During a meeting with the NBA World Champion Philadelphia 76ers]
Larry O'Brien, Commissioner of the NBA: "And I've been told that there are occasions when you do a little refereeing here, and I want to present to you, therefore, an official referee's jacket which you can wear on those occasions when Tip [O'Neill] and the rest come down to visit you. And it is the official referee's jacket. So now you are honorary referee in the NBA, Mr. President."
The President: "Well, I thank you very much. You mean there aren't enough people mad at me already?"

> —*6/8/83*

"And while there's been a certain lack of communication on our part over the years, the other party seems to have capitalized on the rhetoric of compassion. They don't accomplish much, but they sure do talk about it."

—*Remarks at a national Black Republican Council dinner; 9/15/82*

"The finger-pointers and the hand-wringers of today were the policy makers of yesterday, and they gave us economic stagnation and double-digit inflation. There was only one thing fair about their policies: They didn't discriminate; they made everyone miserable."

—*Remarks at the annual convention of the Concrete and Aggregates Industries Associations in Chicago, Ill.; 1/31/84*

"If optimism were a national disease, they'd [liberal critics] be immune for life."

—*Remarks at the annual Conservative Political Action Conference dinner; 3/2/84*

"The critics remind me of the hypochrondriac who was complaining to the doctor. He said, 'My left arm hurts me, and also my left foot, and my back. Oh, and there's my hip and, oh, yes, my neck.' And the doctor muttered something to himself and then sat him down and crossed his legs and tapped him with the little rubber hammer. He says, 'How are you now?' And the patient said, 'Well, now my knee hurts, too.' "

—*Remarks at the annual meeting of the American Medical Association House of Delegates in Chicago, Ill.; 6/23/83*

"What the American people see is that the other party keeps going in circles. And that's just like, you know, when you get lost in the woods; if every time you come to a decision you lean to the left, you will wind up going in circles."

> —*Remarks at a state Republican Party fund-raising dinner; 8/22/85*

"This is the story about a little boy who was selling some puppies that he had to get rid of. And he set up shop right outside a Democratic fund-raiser. And the people began coming out, and one couple stopped and looked, and then, joshingly, the man said, 'Are those Democrat puppies?' And he said, 'Oh, yes, sir.' Well, the couple wound up buying one. Well the next week the Republicans were having a fund-raiser, and he set up shop again—same location and some of the same pups. And out came the people and, sure enough, somebody asked him if they were Republican pups. And he said yes. And he sold one. And a newspaper reporter who was nearby and had been present the week before said, 'Hey, kid, wait a minute. Lask week you said those were Democrat pups. Now you're saying they're Republicans.' And the kid says, 'Yeah.' And the reporter says, 'Well, how come?' He says, 'That's easy. This week they got their eyes open.'"

> —*Remarks at a Nevada Republican Party fund-raising luncheon in Las Vegas, Nev.; 2/7/84*

[Referring to hecklers shouting from the audience]
"You know, I spoke here in 1975 and there wasn't an echo."

> —*Remarks at a luncheon of the World Affairs Council of Philadelphia in Philadelphia, Pa.; 10/15/81*

"Former Congressman Prentiss Walker, who I understand is here today, tells a story about his first campaign. He dropped in on a farm and introduced himself as a Republican candidate. And as he tells it, the farmer's eyes lit up, and then he said, 'Wait till I get my wife. We've never seen a Republican before.' And a few minutes later he was back with his wife, and they asked Prentiss if he wouldn't give them a speech. Well, he looked around for some kind of a podium, something to stand on, and then the only thing available was a pile of that stuff that the late Mrs. Truman said it had taken her thirty-five years to get Harry to call 'fertilizer.' So he stepped up on that and made his speech. And apparently he won them over. And they told him it was the first time they'd ever heard a Republican. And he says, 'That's okay. That's the first time I've ever given a speech from a Democratic platform.'"
     —*Remarks at a Mississippi Republican Party fundraising dinner in Jackson, Miss.; 6/20/83*

"I remember back in the days when, well, when I'd first become a Republican, because I was in the other party. Then, as the Bible says, I put aside childish things."
     —*Remarks at a Senate Republican dinner; 11/21/86*

"Last week Amy Carter was in the news. I'd always thought that if she rebelled it'd mean she'd become a Young Republican."
     —*The annual Gridiron dinner; 4/18/88*

"And when, as a young man, I spent my summers lifeguarding—it wasn't in some posh country club, but on the banks of a river in a small town in northern Illinois. And believe me, there are plenty in the other party who find the

fact that this Republican was born to ordinary working people—they find that kind of hard to take. I've always wondered why it is the Democrats call supporters of the Republican Party 'fat cats,' but their own contributors are called 'public-spirited philanthropists.' "
   —Remarks at a rally for gubernatorial candidate Kay Orr, Omaha, Nebr.; 9/24/86

[To the White House News Photographers' Association]
"There are some things that you and I have in common in addition to being on the opposite ends of the camera. For you, the darkroom is a place to develop film. For me, it's a place the Democrats use as a think tank."
   —5/18/83

"One Democratic congressman who helped engineer the gerrymandering of California once described the district lines there as his contribution to modern art."
   —Remarks at the annual dinner of the Republican Governors Club; 10/15/87

"You know, in 1990 there'll be another reapportionment. And do you know that I believe it's been more than fifty years since Republicans have been in charge of reapportionment. I think in our own state out in California the only Republican district they've left us is south of the border."
   —Remarks to Republican officials; 10/7/85

"An evangelical minister and a politician arrived at Heaven's gate one day together. And St. Peter, after doing all the necessary formalities, took them in hand to show them where their quarters would be. And he took them to a small, single room with a bed, a chair, and a table and said this was for the clergyman. And the politician was a little worried about what might be in store for him. And he couldn't believe it when St. Peter stopped in front of a beautiful mansion with lovely grounds, many servants, and told him that these would be his quarters. And he couldn't help but ask, he said, 'But wait, how—there's something wrong—how do I get this mansion while that good and holy man gets a single room?' And St. Peter said, 'You have to understand how things are up here. We've got thousands and thousands of clergy. You're the first politician who ever made it.'"

  *—Remarks at the annual convention of the National
   Association of Evangelicals in Orlando, Fla.; 3/8/83*

[After a brief period of silence after the President opened up the floor for questions]
"You mean no one has a question? I've got another speech in the other pocket."

  *—Remarks and a question-and-answer session at a
   fund-raising reception in Columbus, Ohio; 10/4/82*

The Evil Empire

"This is a story about General Secretary Gorbachev. It seems that as part of the campaign to straighten things out there in his country he had issued an order that everyone caught speeding, or seen speeding, should get a ticket, no matter how important they might be. Well, one morning he was out at his country home and realized that he was running late for a meeting that he had in the Kremlin. And he went out to get in his car and told the driver to get into the back seat, that he'd drive. And he did, and down the street he went. And they passed two motorcycle policemen, and one of them took off after him. And a little while later, he came back and joined his companion, the other motorcycle officer. And the fellow said, 'Did you give him a ticket?' And he said, 'No.' 'Well,' he said, 'why not?' 'Well,' he said, 'no, no, this was someone too important.' 'Well,' he said, 'we were told to give it no matter who it was, that they would get a—' 'No,' he says, 'not—' 'Well,' he asked, 'who was it?' 'Well,' he said, 'I don't

know. I couldn't recognize him there, but his driver is Gorbachev.' "
> —*Remarks at the swearing-in ceremony for William Verity; 10/19/87*

"A man goes to the official [Soviet automobile] agency, puts down his money and is told that he can take delivery of his automobile in exactly ten years. 'Morning or afternoon?' the purchaser asks. 'Ten years from now, what difference does it make?' replies the clerk. 'Well,' says the car buyer, 'the plumber's coming in the morning.' "
> —*Speech in Santa Barbara, in* The New York Times, *August 21, 1987*

"What are the four things wrong with Soviet agriculture? Spring, summer, winter, and fall."
> —*Remarks at a luncheon hosted by the Rotary Club of West Bend, Wis.; 7/27/87*

"It's like the story of the New Hampshire farmer who had just been to a meeting down in the meeting hall of the local Communist Party. He comes back all excited and tells his friend about how wonderful communism is because, in that system, everyone shares everything they own. 'Does that mean, Fred,' asks his friend, 'that if you had two houses you'd give me one?' 'That's right, John,' he says, 'I'd give you one.' 'And does that mean, Fred, that if you had two tractors you'd give me—' 'That's right, John, if I had two tractors, yes, I'd give you one.' 'Does that mean, Fred, that if you had two hogs you'd give me one?' 'Now that ain't fair, John. You know I got two hogs.' "
> —*Remarks at a White House briefing for business leaders on the Canada-U.S. trade agreement; 11/4/87*

"And George Shultz brought me back one from the Soviet Union the other day. It seems they went in to the General Secretary and told him there was an elderly lady there in the Kremlin who wouldn't leave without seeing him. And he said, 'Well, bring her in.' And they did. And he said, 'Old Mother, what is it? What can I do?' She says, 'I have one question.' She said, 'Was communism invented by a politician or a scientist?' And he said, 'Well, a politician.' She said, 'That explains it. A scientist would have tried it on mice first.'"

—*Remarks at the conference of presidents of major American Jewish organizations; 3/5/86*

"The other day, someone told me the difference between a democracy and a people's democracy. It's the same difference between a jacket and a straitjacket."

—*Remarks by the President at Human Rights Day event; 12/10/86*

"It's about two Soviets who were talking to each other. And one of them asked, 'What's the difference between the Soviet Constitution and the United States Constitution?' And the other one said, 'That's easy. The Soviet Constitution guarantees freedom of speech and freedom of gathering. The American Constitution guarantees freedom *after* speech and freedom *after* gathering.'"

—*Remarks to members of the Community Action Council and the Chamber of Commerce in New Britain, Conn.; 7/8/87*

"How do you tell a Communist? Well, it's someone who reads Marx and Lenin. And how do you tell an anti-

Communist? It's someone who understands Marx and Lenin."
      —*Remarks in Arlington, Va.; 9/25/87*

"Two fellows [are] walking down the street, and one of them says, 'Have we really achieved full communism? Is this it? Is this now full communism?' And the other one said, 'Oh, hell no, things are going to get a lot worse.'"
      —*Remarks at the annual conference of Council of the Americas; 5/21/85*

"You know, they say there are oly two places where communism works: in heaven, where they don't need it and in hell, where they've already got it."
      —*Remarks at a Cuban Independence Day celebration in Miami, Fla.; 5/20/83*

[Asked why there had been little improvement in U.S.-Soviet relations]
"My problem for the first few years was they kept dying on me."
      —*Remarks at a question-and-answer session with regional journalists; 9/16/85*

[Commenting on his zero option proposal, which called for the elimination of all intermediate nuclear missiles by both parties]
"And I may say, the news is encouraging. The Soviet Union has met us halfway on the zero option. They've agreed to zero on our part."
      —*Remarks at the recommissioning ceremony for the U.S.S. New Jersey in Long Beach, Calif.; 12/28/82*

"Brezhnev, before he died, was supposed to be talking to a Russian general. And he said to the general, 'I liked the arms race better when we were the only ones in it.'"

—*Question-and-answer session with high school students on domestic and foreign policy issues; 1/21/83*

"There's an underground joke that's told in the Soviet Union, for example, about a teacher who asked one of the young students, Ivan, what life is like in the United States. And dutifully Ivan said, 'Half the people are unemployed and millions are hungry or starving.' 'Well, then,' the teacher asks, 'then what is the goal of the Soviet Union?' Ivan said, 'To catch up with the United States.'"

—*Remarks by the President at the Conservative Political Action Committee luncheon; 2/20/87*

"And there's a story about a Russian and an American who were talking about the freedoms in their countries; and the American said, 'Listen, in America,' he said, "I can stand on any street corner or out in the park anyplace I want and openly criticize the President of the United States.' And the Russian said, 'We have the same privilege in the Soviet Union.' And the American was pretty surprised. The Russian said, 'I can stand on any street corner in any park in Russia, and I can openly criticize the President of the United States.'"

—*Remarks on presenting the Small Business Person of the Year Award; 5/9/84*

"[There was] a spat between a Soviet and an American over whose country has more freedom. The American boasted that America is so free, he'd urinated on the President's car. That's nothing, said the Soviet, I defecated on the general secretary's limo. The American was amazed, and sheepishly admitted that the President wasn't in the car at the time. Well, said the Soviet, to be honest I didn't take my pants off."

> —*As told by Fred Barnes, in* The New Republic, *December 7, 1987*

[Referring to recent protests in Poland]
"Three dogs were having a conversation: an American dog, a Polish dog, and a Russian dog. And the American dog was telling them about how he barks and that in our country his master gives him some meat. And the Polish dog says, 'What's meat?' And the Russian dog says, 'What's bark?'"

> —*Remarks on signing the Bill of Rights Day and Human Rights Day and Week proclamation; 12/9/83*

[To members of the American Association of Editorial Cartoonists]
"If someone were to ask what's the difference between the United States and the Soviet Union, I guess one answer would be that in the United States editorial cartoonists can publish pictures lampooning Ronald Reagan, while in the Soviet Union cartoonists *must* publish pictures lampooning Ronald Reagan."

> —*5/7/87*

"If the Soviet Union let another political party come into existence, they would still be a one-party state, because everybody'd join the other party."

> —*Remarks to Polish Americans in Chicago, Ill.; 6/23/83*

"There's a story of a dissident who, when he was sentenced to a labor camp in one of those countries, complained to the judge that his sentence was too light. He said, 'If the United States is as bad as you say it is, send me there.'"

—*Remarks at Captive Nations Week; 7/21/86*

"Castro was making a speech to a large audience, and he said, 'They say that I am—accuse me of intervening in Angola.' And a man going through the audience said, 'Peanuts, popcorn!' Castro said, 'They say that I'm intervening in Mozambique,' and the same voice said, 'Peanuts and popcorn!' And he said, 'They say I'm intervening in Nicaragua.' 'Peanuts and popcorn!' And by this time he's boiling mad, and he said, 'Bring me that man who's shouting "peanuts and popcorn" to me, and I'm going to kick him all the way to Miami.' And everybody in the audience started shouting, 'Peanuts and popcorn!'"

—*Remarks at the annual convention of the U.S. Hispanic Chamber of Commerce in Tampa, Fla.; 8/12/83*

"But the story I'm thinking of concerns a star Soviet athlete, a hammer thrower. He'd gone to the West and seen what it was like and then returned home. And in the first meet after he got back, he set a new world record. A journalist from a Soviet newspaper rushed up to him and asked, 'Comrade, how did you manage to throw your hammer that far?' And he replied, 'Give me a sickle, and I'll throw it even further.'"

—*Remarks at a luncheon hosted by the Rotary Club of West Bend, Wis.; 7/27/87*

"This is a story of a commissar who visited one of [the Soviets'] collective farms, and he stopped the first farmer, workman, that he met, and he asked about life on the farm. And the man said, 'It's wonderful. I've never heard anyone complain about anything since I've been here.' And the commissar then said, 'Well, what about the crops?' 'Oh,' he said, 'the crops are wonderful.' 'What about the potatoes?' 'Oh, sir,' he said, 'the potatoes,' he said, 'there are so many that if we put them in one pile they would touch the foot of God.' And the commissar said, 'Just a minute. In the Soviet Union there is no God.' And the farmer said, 'Well, there are no potatoes either.'"

—*Remarks at a Cuban Independence Day celebration, Miami, Fla.; 5/20/83*

"There's a story, incidentally, about a May Day parade in Moscow. First came the tanks and then the armored personnel carriers and the artillery and the missiles and then the marching troops with fixed bayonets, and finally at the end a black sedan with red flags flying and filled with men in grey suits. And a visitor from our part of the world who was there for the occasion asked a local citizen, 'What is that?' And the fellow said, 'That's our most lethal weapon. They're Socialist economists.'"

—*Remarks at the campaign for the 100th Congress; 3/10/86*

"By the way, did you hear that the Communists now have a million-dollar lottery for their people? The winners get a dollar a year for a million years."

—*Remarks at the annual convention of the Veterans of Foreign Wars in New Orleans, La.; 8/15/83*

"What is a Soviet historian? Someone who can accurately predict the past."
> —*Remarks to the New Jersey State Chamber of Commerce, Somerset, N.J.; 10/13/87*

"This is also the night of the Kremlin Correspondents' dinner in Moscow. That's when the members of the Soviet media gather to laugh at Gorbachev's jokes—or else."
> —*Remarks at the annual White House Correspondents' Association dinner; 4/17/86*

"In Russia, if you say 'Take my wife—please,' you come home and she is gone."
> *Speech in Santa Barbara, Calif., August 21, 1987*

"A man just back from Europe, riding in a taxicab—the taxicab driver said to him, 'There is the tallest building in Moscow.' And he looked out, and he said, 'Well, where? Where is it?' He said, 'There, that building.' And this American said, 'That two-story building is the tallest building in Moscow?' He says, 'Yes, from there you can see all the way to Siberia. It's KGB headquarters.'"
> —*Remarks to the fortieth anniversary conference of the United States Advisory Commission on Public Diplomacy; 9/16/87*

"We've just learned that from now on KGB agents have been ordered to do all their work in groups of three: One agent to take notes and write the report and the other two to keep an eye on the intellectual."
> —*Remarks at dedication ceremonies for new facilities, National Security Agency; 9/26/86*

"But the Soviets have really gone too far. It's no secret that I wear a hearing aid. Well, just the other day, all of a sudden, it went haywire. We discovered the KGB had put a listening device in my listening device."

—Remarks at the annual dinner of the White House Correspondents' Association; 4/22/87

"Evening, or darkness, in the Soviet Union. A citizen walking along the street. A soldier yells 'Halt.' He starts to run, the soldier shoots him. Another citizen says, 'Why did you do that?' And the soldier says, "Curfew.' 'But,' he said, 'it isn't curfew time yet.' He said, 'I know. He's a friend of mine. I know where he lives. He couldn't have made it.'"

—Remarks in a meeting of the Executive Exchange Committee; 10/6/86

"There's a story of a diplomat who caught a taxi in Washington, and on the long ride to Dulles International Airport, he struck up a conversation with the cabbie. And the young man happened to mention that he would be graduating in a few weeks. And the diplomat asked what kind of work he intended to pursue. 'I don't know,' replied the cabbie, 'because I haven't decided yet.' Well, once at Dulles, the diplomat caught a plane which was taking him straight to the Soviet Union, to Moscow. And arriving there, he got in a taxicab and started the long ride in, and he, speaking fluent Russian, struck up a conversation with that cabbie. The cabbie, by coincidence, said he too would soon be graduating. And when the diplomat asked him what line of work he planned to pursue, the cabbie replied, 'I don't know; *they* haven't decided yet.'"

—Remarks at the Tuskegee Institute commencement ceremony; 5/10/87

"My fellow Americans, I am pleased to tell you I have signed legislation to outlaw Russia forever. We begin bombing in five minutes."
 —*Radio voice check, August 12, 1984*

Public Enemy #1
(The U.S. Government)

"Let me welcome you to Washington, and I know that Nancy joins me in this. And welcome to the twilight zone. I should warn you that things in this city aren't often the way they seem. Where but in Washington would they call the department that's in charge of everything outdoors, everything outside, the Department of Interior."

—Remarks at a fund-raising dinner for the Republican National Hispanic Assembly; 9/14/83

"You know, sometimes there are two ways of doing things: the right way, and the way they do it in Washington."

—Remarks at the Cenikor Foundation Center in Houston, Tex.; 4/29/83

"You know, it's said that the ten most frightening words in the English language are: 'Hello, I'm from the government and I'm here to help.'"

—Remarks at a White House briefing for representatives of the small business community; 10/29/87

"Some people have labored so long to make government bigger that they've developed a knee-jerk addiction to tax increases, and every time their knee jerks, we get kicked."
—*Remarks at a fund-raising luncheon for Senator Don Nickles of Oklahoma; 6/5/85*

"There are some in government who have a very simple tax proposal in mind. There will only be two lines on the tax form: How much did you make last year? Send it."
—*Remarks during a meeting with Puerto Rican leaders; 3/15/84*

"You know, I've never been very good, myself, at fundraising. And I've told some of my friends on occasion that—that that's why I got in government, because we don't ask for it, we just take it."
—*Remarks at the awards presentation ceremony for the President's Committee on the Arts and Humanities; 5/17/83*

". . . government's view of the economy could be summed up in a few short phrases: If it moves, tax it. If it keeps moving, regulate it. And if it stops moving, subsidize it."
—*Remarks to the White House Conference on Small Business; 8/15/86*

"You know, there's been a lot of jousting and hustling going on there across the river in the Capital. You learn that when you get between the hog and the bucket, you get jousted about a bit."
—*Remarks at a fund-raising luncheon for Virginia gubernatorial candidate Wyatt Durette; 10/9/85*

"Status quo, you know, that is Latin for 'the mess we're in.'"

—*Remarks at a reception for members of the Associated General Contractors of America; 3/16/81*

"If the Congress wants to bring the Panamanian economy to its knees, why doesn't it just go down there and run the country."

—*Remarks at the annual Gridiron Dinner, 4/26/88*

"You know, the choices are very simple for us. You can't go in and instantly clean out the stable and change things that have been piling up for as many years as they have."

—*Remarks at a Kansas Republican fund-raising luncheon in Topeka, Kans.; 9/9/82*

". . . ranchers and herders . . . they have exactly the same sort of disposal problems in that business that we have in politics."

—*Remarks at a dinner honoring Senator Paul Laxalt of Nevada; 3/3/86*

". . . far too often, people with talent think the only way to better their country is to immerse themselves in politics. Some even delude themselves into thinking that political contributions are gifts of charity. In fact, some of the politicians think that."

—*Remarks at the annual Ambassadors Ball to benefit the Multiple Sclerosis Society; 9/22/81*

"Unfortunately, in the last two decades we've experienced an onslaught of such twisted logic that if Alice were visit-

ing America, she might think she'd never left Won-
derland."

   —*Remarks at a candle-lighting ceremony for prayer*
      in schools; 9/25/82

"We're suffering the worst inflation in sixty years. Almost
eight billion . . . million, million Americans are continuing
to be out of work. I've been here only a month and I'm
beginning to talk in billions when I mean millions."

   —*Remarks at the Mid-Winter Congressional City*
      Conference of the National League of Cities; 3/2/81

"Taxation has been called the art of plucking the feathers
without killing the bird, but before we got there the folks in
Washington didn't seem to know when to stop the plucking."

   —*Remarks at a Nevada Republican rally in Las*
      Vegas; 10/28/82

"Well, that's their answer to just about every problem—
rob Peter to pay Paul. They don't realize Peter went back-
rupt a long time ago."

   —*Remarks in New Orleans, La.; 3/27/86*

"The American taxing structure, the purpose of which was
to serve the people, began instead to serve the insatiable
appetite of government. If you will forgive me, you know
someone has once likened government to a baby. It is an
alimentary canal with an appetite at one end and no sense
of responsibility at the other."

   —*Remarks before a joint session of Parliament in*
      Ottawa, Canada; 3/11/81

"If I could paraphrase Will Rogers' line about never having met a man he didn't like, it seems that some in government have never met a tax they didn't hike."
   —*Remarks in Los Angeles at the luncheon of the Central City and California Taxpayer's Association; 6/25/81*

"You have to see it to believe it. There in one box it tells you your gross pay. And then you have all those other boxes with the taxes taken out."
   —*Remarks to the students and faculty of North Carolina State University; 9/5/85*

[After being told by aide Lyn Nofziger shortly after his shooting that everything in Washington was "running normally"]
"What makes you think I'd be happy about that?"
   —*4/1/81*

"Like the story of the man from Jefferson Parish—he sent a letter to the IRS saying: 'Enclosed is a check for $1,000. I cheated on my taxes last year, and I can't sleep at night. P.S. If I still can't sleep, I'll send you the rest I owe you.'"
   —*Remarks in New Orleans, La.; 9/18/86*

"In addition to long-term reforms of spending, I believe we should make our tax system more simple, fair, and rewarding for all the people. Would you believe I've been told that even Albert Einstein had to ask the IRS for help on his 1040?"
   —*Remarks at a Spirit of America rally in Atlanta, Ga.; 1/26/84*

"They say that money talks, well, a few years ago the only thing it said was good-bye."

—*Remarks at a fund-raising dinner for Senator Mack Mattingly of Georgia; 6/5/85*

"But just as everything is starting to mesh, just as Americans have spotted the dawn of a new age—strong growth without a return to runaway inflation and interest rates—the guardians of the graveyard philosophy want to resurrect ideas which should remain dead and buried for all time. They have a kind of layaway plan for your lives which never changes. It's called, 'Americans make, government takes.'"

—*Remarks at the national conference of the National Federation of Independent Business; 6/22/83*

"Our critics have spent a lot of time trying to find a cloud to go with the silver lining. The silver lining has been one of the longest peacetime expansions in the past forty years. But in the process, they've been getting things so mixed up that they remind me of that teacher who asked her students which is more important, the sun or the moon? And one little boy raised his hand and said, 'The moon, because the sun's around during the day when you don't need it. And if it wasn't for the moon, it'd be totally dark at night."

—*Remarks in Washington, D.C.; 5/1/87*

"Now, there are those who oppose the bipartisan tax cut, because frankly they're afraid the government will lose revenue. Now, somehow that doesn't strike me as a national disaster."

—*Remarks in Chicago, Ill.; 7/7/81*

"I know that even as far away as Missouri you've been hearing the howls coming from Washington about Gramm-Rudman-Hollings. The gloom and doomers are talking as though it'll close down the entire federal government. Hmmmmm."
    —*Remarks in St. Louis, Mo.; 2/12/86*

"And I remember about the third time that we did that, a long-time senator, state senator, came into my office one day outraged about our giving that money back to the people. And he said he considered giving that money back to the people an unnecessary expenditure of public funds."
    —*Remarks during a roundtable discussion with housing industry representatives in Arlington, Tex.; 4/12/84*

"You know, not too long ago, I was asked to explain the difference between a small businessman and a big businessman. And my answer was that a big businessman is what a small businessman would be if only the government would get out of the way and leave him alone."
    —*Remarks on presenting the Small Business Person of the Year award; 5/9/84*

"There is a great reluctance on the part of the federal government to trust the people out there, and they believe that inhaling the fogs off the Potomac imparts a wisdom that is not generally shared."
    —*Remarks and a question-and-answer session with state and local officials during a White House briefing on the Program for Economic Recovery; 5/28/81*

"You know, it's a pleasure to be able to travel such a short distance and still come so far from the Washington state of mind. On this side of the river, only horses suffer from Potomac fever."

> —*Remarks at a Virginia Republican Party rally in Richmond; 9/29/82*

"Sometimes I can't help thinking of people like you as emissaries from the real world—the great land that lies beyond the Potomac where a special interest is a hobby like fishing, and a lobbyist is someone who hangs around a hotel."

> —*Remarks at a meeting with state and local officials; 6/27/85*

"You know, when you mention common sense in Washington, you cause a kind of traumatic shock."

> —*Remarks at a Republican rally in Irving, Tex.; 10/11/82*

"I've always thought that the common sense and wisdom of government were summed up in a sign they used to have hanging on that gigantic Hoover Dam. It said, 'Government property. Do not remove.'"

> —*Remarks at the nineteenth annual meeting of the National Alliance of Business; 9/14/87*

". . . common sense is about as common in Washington, D.C., as a Fourth of July blizzard in Columbia, South Carolina."

> —*Remarks in Columbia, S. Car.; 9/20/83*

[Commenting on the Aberdeen Central High School choir, which traveled to Washington for the January 1985 presidential inauguration, which was partially canceled due to cold weather]

"These young people, all of them—well, this group trekked all the way to Washington to perform at the inaugural only to be thwarted by cold weather. Who would have thought that in Washington, with all the hot air that blows in that town, cold weather could be an obstacle?"
  —*Remarks in Sioux Falls, S. Dak.; 9/29/86*

[To a crowd in Minneapolis, Minnesota]
"Well, we had some terrible snowstorms in Washington this year, too. But it didn't really last there. As you know, we have a lot more hot air blowers."
  —*6/9/83*

"There are pressures in Washington that make a Las Vegas crap table look like an oasis of calm."
  —*Remarks in Las Vegas, Nev.; 6/25/86*

". . . there's a difficult thing about cutting expenses—the expenses can vote."
  —*Remarks on presenting a check for the Westway highway project to Mayor Koch in New York; 9/7/81*

"Sometimes government reminds me of the lady who ran a pretzel stand just outside an office building. Every day a fellow who was in that office building would stop by her stand, and he'd put a quarter in her plate. And he never took a pretzel. And every day, the same thing—he'd put a quarter on the plate, and never take the pretzel. And then one day he put a quarter on the plate, and she grabbed him by the arm. He said, 'You probably want to know why I've been putting twenty-five cents on your plate every day for the last year and have never taken a pretzel.' And she said, 'No, I just wanted to tell you pretzels are thirty-five cents now.'"

    —*Remarks to the National White House Conference on Small Business; 12/23/86*

"A government agency is the nearest thing to eternal life we'll ever see on this Earth."

    —*Remarks at Eureka College in Eureka, Ill.; 2/6/84*

"But you know, sometimes these government programs, it's a little bit like the story of the country preacher who called on a town about one hundred miles away from his own. He went there for a revival meeting. And on the way to the church, he noticed in that town that sitting on the porch of a little country store was a man from his own hometown, a fellow that was known for his drinking. And the minister went up to him and asked what he was doing so far from home. 'Preacher,' he said, 'beer is five cents a bottle cheaper here.' The minister told him that didn't make much sense—the expense of traveling all that way and back, the price of lodging and all while he was there. The drinker thought for a moment and then replied, 'Preacher, I'm not stupid. I just sit here and drink till I show a profit.'"

    —*Remarks in Louisville, Ky.; 10/7/83*

"Accepting a government grant with its accompanying rules is like marrying a girl and finding out her entire family is moving in with you before the honeymoon."

>—*Remarks at the annual convention of the National Conference of State Legislatures in Atlanta, Ga.; 7/30/81*

". . . when I think about regulations, I always remember one of the favorite stories I had about bureaucracy long before I was here in Washington. [There] was a fellow here in Washington that sat at a desk, and papers came to him, and he looked at them and decided where they should go, initialed them, and sent them on. And one day a classified document arrived at his desk. Well, he accepted it, saw where it should go, initialed it, sent it on. Twenty-four hours later, it came back to him. It said, 'You weren't supposed to see this. Erase your initials and initial the erasure.' "

>—*Remarks on signing the annual report on the state of small business; 3/19/84*

"The state of Wyoming turned down a juvenile justice grant because it would have cost the state five hundred thousand dollars in compliance to get a two-hundred-thousand-dollar grant. You remember that old gag we used to pull, 'Have you got two tens for a five?' The city of San Diego built a sixteen-mile trolley without federal assistance, which is probably why it was accomplished within the budget and on time. I wish I could interest San Diego in taking over Amtrak."

>—*Remarks at the annual convention of the National Conference of State Legislatures in Atlanta, Ga.; 7/30/81*

"You know, the difference between local government and Washington is very simple. Recently, there was a little town. Their traffic signs were only five feet high, and they decided to raise them, for better visibility for the motorists, to raise them to seven feet above the ground. And the federal government came in and said they had a program that would do that for them. They lowered the pavement two feet."

—*Remarks in Los Angeles, Calif.; 8/17/81*

"You know, a fellow comes in, stands in front of your desk, hands you a memorandum, and he stays and waits there while you read it. And so you read: 'Action-oriented orchestration, innovation, inputs generated by escalation of meaningful, indigenous decision-making dialogue, focusing on multilinked problem complexes, can maximize the vital thrust toward nonaligned and viable urban infrastructure.' I take a chance and say, 'Let's try busing.' And if he walks away, I know I guessed right."

—*Remarks at a reception honoring* The National Review; *2/21/83*

". . . if we mean to continue governing, [we] must realize that it will not always be so easy to place the blame on the past for our national difficulties. You know, one day the great baseball manager Frankie Frisch sent a rookie out to play center field. The rookie promptly dropped the first fly ball that was hit to him. On the next play he let a grounder go between his feet and then threw the ball to the wrong base. Frankie stormed out of the dugout, took his glove away from him, and said, 'I'll show you how to play this position.' And the next batter slammed a line drive right over second base. Frankie came in on it, missed it com-

pletely, fell down when he tried to chase it, threw down his glove, and yelled at the rookie, 'You've got center field so screwed up nobody can play it.' "
    —*Remarks at the Conservative Political Action Conference dinner; 3/20/81*

"Now, I don't question others' good intentions. I've simply noticed there's a well-known road that's paved with good intentions, but no one wants to go where it would take you."
    —*Remarks at a fund-raising luncheon for Senator Don Nickles; 6/5/85*

"The time has come to rethink some of the tired old political labels that have blinded our thinking for too long. You know, we Americans have the technological genius to send astronauts to the moon and bring them safely home, but we're having trouble making it safe for a citizen to take a walk in the evening through the park. And sometimes in the world of politics, it seems that your dialogue hasn't gone much beyond 'Me Tarzan, you Jane.' "
    —*Remarks at Kansas State University at the Alfred M. Landon lecture series; 9/9/82*

"And now, I'm delighted to sign the executive order creating the first Presidential Advisory Commission on Women's Business Ownership. [After the first pen fails to write] It's a funny thing, these government pens. It takes three of them to write one name."
    —*Remarks at the national conference of the National Federation of Independent Business; 6/22/83*

"But you know, talking about some of the problems in Washington right now is a little like the Irish landlady who put up a lunch every day for one of her boarders that he took to work. And he was always unhappy about the lunch and let her know when he came home. So, she put two slices of bread in, and the next day she put in four, and he was still unhappy. And then she put in six, and he was unhappy. She got up to about ten, and he was still griping about the quantity of the lunch, so she split a loaf of bread, and put that in the lunch. He came home, and she was waiting for him and said, 'How was the lunch?' He said, 'Well, all right, but I see you're back to two slices again.' "

    —Remarks in New Orleans, La.; 9/28/81

[After an opening prayer]
"I don't know of a place where prayer is more appropriate than in Washington, D.C."

    —Remarks at a White House luncheon for officials of black colleges and universities; 9/15/81

Public Enemy #2
(The Press)

"It's my job to solve all the country's problems and it's your job to make sure no one finds out about it."
> —*Remarks to the White House Correspondents' Association dinner; 1985*

[On Sam Donaldson]
"Somebody asked me one day why we didn't put a stop to Sam's shouting out questions at us when we're out on the South Lawn. We can't. If we did, the starlings would come back."
> —*Remarks at the annual awards dinner of the White House News Photographers' Association; 5/18/83*

"I have to admit we considered making one final shipment to Iran, but no one could figure out how to get Sam Donaldson in a crate."
> —*Remarks to the White House Correspondents' Association dinner; 4/27/87*

"I heard that Lesley Stahl [CBS News] has been asking if anything can be done to improve my answers. Yes, ask better questions."
   —*Remarks at the annual dinner of the White House Correspondents' Association; 4/13/84*

"Incidentally, I've got a news item for you: We have a spinoff from our Star Wars research. It's a helmet for me to wear at press conferences. All I do is push a button and it shoots down incoming questions."
   —*Remarks at the annual Gridiron Dinner; 4/28/87*

Journalist: "You wouldn't turn down our invitation to come talk to us, would you, Mr. President?"
The President: "If I can choose the subjects, no."
   —*Remarks on greeting the New York Islanders; 5/24/83*

"Well, I'm looking forward to the next news conference. I have so many questions to ask you all."
   —*Remarks by telephone to the annual dinner of the White House Correspondents' Association; 4/25/81*

"Nancy's taken to watching the press conferences, and now every time I answer a question, she says, 'I have a follow-up.'"
   —*Remarks at the annual dinner of the White House Correspondents' Association; 4/13/84*

"But do you know what it's like to have Chris Wallace and Bill Plante screaming questions in your ear when you're only about ten feet from the helicopter with the motor roaring, and you realize they're asking, 'What's wrong with your hearing, Mr. President?' "

   —*Remarks at the annual dinner of the White House Correspondents' Association; 4/13/84*

"We have installed one new feature [in the new White House briefing room]. The place is wired for sound. We can press a button here on the podium and get instant helicopter noise here."

   —*Remarks at the reopening of the press briefing room at the White House; 11/9/81*

"Well, aren't we overwhelmed by the grandeur of the place? First, let me welcome all you orphans home. You know, we sort of missed you. It's been quiet over here, kind of like when the kids go back to school."

   —*Remarks at the reopening of the press briefing room at the White House; 11/9/81*

[After reports appeared that Libyan assassination squads had been sent to assassinate the President]
Question: "Do you feel you're adequately protected?"
The President: "Yes. If I didn't think I was adequately protected, I wouldn't come in this [press] room."

   —*Exchange with reporters; 12/7/81*

[After Nancy offers pieces of the President's birthday cake to journalists]
Journalist: "But you understand, we won't sell out for a piece of cake. No deals."
The President: "Oh, you've sold out for less than that."

   —*Remarks and a question-and-answer session with reporters on domestic and foreign policy issues; 2/4/83*

Question: "I'd like to ask you, sir, your own views after the fact on the decision not to have press at the Grenada action, and if that happened again, do you think that would be the policy to follow again?"

The President: "Now, I won't do—in any operation of the same kind, I won't do what someone suggested, and that is that, yes sir, we guarantee the press go along, and we put them right in the front row of the landing barges, so they'll be first off."

> *—Remarks and a question-and-answer session with editors of Gannett Newspapers on domestic and foreign policy issues; 12/14/83*

Helen Thomas: "Thank you. Are you—"

The President: "What?"

Helen Thomas: "Did you want to answer the first part [of my question]?"

The President: "Oh, the first part of the question. I knew there was—I talked too long on that other part. And the first part is—all I can say is: Tune in next week. I will be speaking to the subject of our disarmament proposals and so forth next week. But there's nothing to comment on today."

Helen Thomas: "Thank you."

The President: "Helen said, 'thank you.'"

Other reporter: "You can overrule her if you want. You're the President. You're the boss."

The President: "Helen, you never told me that."

> *—Exchange with reporters; 3/25/83*

"Gee, all of these cameras are on my bad side."

> *—Remarks and a question-and-answer session with regional editors and broadcasters on domestic and foreign policy issues; 2/9/83*

[To the White House News Photographers' Association]
"And, if we'll all just remember, my best side is my right
side—my far right side."
—*5/18/83*

"I'm told that there's a feeling among photographers that
journalists don't treat you well or as fairly as you'd like.
Welcome to the club."
—*Remarks at the annual awards dinner for the White
House News Photographers' Association; 5/18/83*

"You know, I like your White House photographers motto,
'One picture is worth a thousand denials.' "
—*Remarks at the annual awards dinner for the White
House News Photographers' Association; 5/18/83*

"Just the other day, I saw my first robin redbreast of the
spring in a tree outside the Oval Office—and six of you in
the bushes."
—*Remarks at the annual awards dinner for the White
House News Photographers' Association; 5/18/83*

"I want to tell you, though, I had a bad moment—or
Nancy and I did when we came in here. You're all so
beautifully dressed and dressed up that we thought maybe
we'd gotten to the wrong dinner."
—*Remarks at the annual awards dinner for the White
House News Photographers' Association; 5/18/83*

"But on the level, though, I like photographers. You don't
ask questions."
—*Remarks at the annual awards dinner for the White
House News Photographers' Association; 5/18/83*

"Can you imagine Sam Donaldson with a camera? As most of you would say, 'The thought makes me shutter.'"
—*Remarks at the annual awards dinner for the White House News Photographers' Association; 5/18/83*

"The public depends on you to keep them informed about what we're really doing here and expects you to keep an eye on the presidency. And, Sam [Donaldson], that doesn't mean you can put a ladder up to the third-floor windows."
—*Remarks at the reopening of the press briefing room at the White House; 11/9/81*

[After reports that the President always first pointed at female reporters dressed in red during questions at his press conferences]
"At my last press conference, I thought that gimmick of wearing a red dress to get my attention went a little too far, but it was a nice try, Sam."
—*Remarks at the annual dinner of the White House Correspondents' Association; 4/17/86*

"I understand ABC's having some budget problems. The news division has already laid off three hair stylists. Well, they weren't alone. That sweater Dan Rather wears came from Goodwill Industries."
—*Remarks at the annual dinner of the White House Correspondents' Association; 4/17/86*

"Incidentally, I know that some of you talk a little bit, and you're critical about what you say is my 'living in the past.' But I think that's because a lot of you just don't realize how

good the old days were. You know, then you looked forward to seeing Lana Turner in a sweater, not Dan Rather."
> —*Remarks at the annual dinner of the White House*
> *Correspondents' Association; 4/13/84*

Question: "Do you think the public has anything to complain about in terms of what it is getting in the way of news
out of Washington in your administration?"
The President: "Yes. I'd like to see the press complain that
they're getting too many leaks."
> —*Interview with* USA Today; *4/26/83*

"Sometimes I read memos in the paper that I haven't
gotten yet."
> —*Remarks and a question-and-answer session with*
> *editors of Gannett Newspapers on domestic and*
> *foreign policy issues; 12/14/83*

"I guess when there isn't any real news, you pick rumors."
> —*After remarks to women leaders of Christian reli-*
> *gious organizations; 10/13/83*

"Well, now, I couldn't help noticing something about the
kind remark that [President Thomas] Jefferson made about
the press. He made it *before* he was President, not during
his term."
> —*Remarks on signing the World Communications*
> *Year proclamation; 12/16/82*

Mr. d'Arbeloff: "This really concludes our presentation,
Mr. President. Since we are speaking without the press
present, we thought we might have a question-and-answer
period."

The President [noting a number of photojournalists present in the audience]: "Well, that's just fine with me. All right. I see you have a couple of camera clubs, though, that dropped in."

—Remarks and a question-and-answer session with members of the Massachusetts High Technology Council in Bedford, Mass.; 1/26/83

Question: "Could I go back to Libya again, Mr. President? Your spokesman this morning—"
The President: "Be careful when you go there."

—Interview with journalists representing nations participating in the Tokyo economic summit; 4/22/86

"I hope Leonid Brezhnev can come to New York in June. I want him to see our free press in action. I want him to see that contrast between a free press and a controlled press, that's the only thing he knows. They can't criticize him, they can't take potshots, write insulting stories about him when he takes a day off to go swimming. . . . On the other hand, there's something to be said for a controlled press."

—The annual Gridiron Dinner; 4/21/82

The Right Staff

"Welcome to the White House. I told some people the other day that Nancy and I managed to be very happy here, in spite of having a hundred MXs in the basement."
—*Remarks to state and local officials on proposed federalism legislation; 2/24/83*

"Thank you for a very warm welcome. It's a pleasure for me to break away from crisis negotiations. You're the first to know this. I've just called in Ambassador Phil Habib to settle the Jim Watt–Beach Boy controversy."
—*Remarks to members of the National Catholic Educational Association; 4/7/83*

"Delighted to have you all here this morning. Maybe some of you noticed the helicopter was on the lawn in case my reception was somewhat different than it's been."
—*Remarks and question-and-answer session on the Program for Economic Recovery at a breakfast for newspaper and television news editors; 2/19/81*

"I want you to know that I don't expect every morning to
be greeted by the Marine Band."
  —*Remarks at the inauguration day ceremony for
  members of the White House staff; 1/23/81*

"Vice President Bush, Attorney General Meese, and President William Falsgraf of the American Bar Association
and the presidents of the National Bar Association and the
Federal Bar Association—good morning to all of you and
welcome to the White House complex. The White House
complex is what you get when you have been working here
too long."
  —*Remarks at a White House Law Day ceremony;
  4/16/86*

"When I was a very small boy in a small town in Illinois,
we lived above the store where my father worked. I have
something of the same arrangement here."
  —*Remarks on presenting the Small Business Person
  of the Year award; 5/11/83*

"I'm delighted to be here today—and by the way, I mentioned to General Odom and Bill Casey the unseasonably
warm weather predictions for today, but they told me to
wear my trench coat anyway. And then when I asked for
directions to this great new building, all they would say is:
'Mr. President, leave the White House, go to Seventeenth
and K, and wait for the phone to ring.'"
  —*Remarks at the dedication ceremonies for new facil-
  ities, National Security Agency; 9/26/86*

"You know, when I first started in my present job, I'd
sometimes put together in my mind my own dream Cabi-

net—you know, John Wayne as Secretary of State, Clint
Eastwood at Defense, Jack Benny as Secretary of Trea-
sury, Grouch Marx at Education.''
   —Remarks at the all-star tribute to Dutch Reagan,
   Burbank, Calif.; 12/1/85

"And yet, even at the start of the administration, people
like Jeane Kirkpatrick were offering some pretty broad
hints that things would be different. 'How will the Reagan
administration change American foreign policy?' she was
asked early in 1981 at the United Nations. She answered
correctly. She said, 'Well, we've taken down our "Kick
me" sign.' And then someone said, 'Well does that mean
that if the United States is kicked it will kick back?' 'Not
necessarily,' she said. 'But it does mean we won't apolo-
gize.'"
   —Remarks at the Heritage Foundation's tenth anni-
   versary dinner; 4/22/86

"There's been some criticism, however, that we don't have
a definite foreign policy, that we haven't been doing enough
about that, and that's not true at all. Just the other day,
before he left for China, Al Haig sent a message to
Brezhnev that said, 'Roses are red, violets are blue, stay
out of El Salvador, and Poland, too.'"
   —Remarks at a White House reception for the Re-
   publican National Committee; 6/12/81

"I received another letter from Gorbachev today. He proposed holding American-style elections in the USSR,
opening his borders for free movement of people, estab-
lishing an independent news media, and tearing down the
Berlin Wall. Pat Buchanan dismissed it as nothing new."
   —Remarks at the annual White House Correspon-
   dents' Association dinner; 4/17/86

"The old Deaver rule was 'no questions.' The new Buchanan rule is 'no answers.'"

> *—Remarks at the annual White House Correspondents' Association dinner; 1985*

"Sam Pierce, Secretary of Housing and Urban Development, already proved his quality in some of the meetings we've been having. He found the only washbasin in the washroom that you could get hot water out of."

> *—Remarks on signing the federal employee hiring freeze memorandum and the Cabinet member nominations; 1/20/81*

Bob Pierpoint: "Mr. President, this is Bob Pierpoint at the podium."
The President: "Bob, I hope you don't mind, but David Stockman is making me call collect."

> *—Remarks by telephone at the annual dinner of the White House Correspondents' Association; 4/25/81*

Question: "How about these heartless budget cuts?"
The President [pointing to his aides]: "Back to you."

> *—Remarks during a White House briefing on the Program for Economic Recovery; 2/24/81*

" . . . we've succeeded in getting our budget cuts through Congress. I worried for a while when that happened that maybe Dave Stockman was too young—he rushed right out and got a giant piggybank."

> *—Remarks at a White House reception for the Republican National Committee; 6/12/81*

"For those who might be in the back, my desk is now an old door on four cement blocks, a crate for a seat, and my pens are kept in an empty bean can. So I have just written, 'Dear Dave [Stockman], I hope you can use second-hand cement blocks. The price of concrete is out of sight.'"
    —*Remarks on signing documents transmitting budget revision to the Congress; 3/9/81*

"Also, our summer youth employment program has a budget of more than eight hundred million dollars—an increase of a hundred million dollars over last year—to provide more than eight hundred thousand summer jobs for young people throughout the United States. In fact, just last week here in the Rose Garden we found another eight hundred thousand dollars—well, we didn't find it in the Rose Garden. . . . We're not that careless! We found it over at the Labor Department."
    —*Remarks at a White House reception for the National Council of Negro Women; 7/28/83*

"Incidentally, did you see our friend Lyn Nofziger on '60 Minutes' the other night? They said that he is our influence peddler. That's ridiculous. He just dresses like a peddler."
    —*Remarks at the annual White House Correspondents' Association dinner; 1982*

"For the ladies present, having referred to that rough and ready Teddy Roosevelt a couple of times, I think you ought to know that in that era, there was no West Wing to the White House and the East Wing. All the offices and the Cabinet meetings and everything else took place there in the residence. And then one day, Mrs. Roosevelt proved to be a match. She said to the President of the United States,

'If I'm going to raise six kids in this house, you're going to get your people out of here.'"

—*Remarks to the American Legion Washington Leadership Conference; 2/10/87*

"Nancy is sorry that she couldn't be here, and so am I. She sent her warm regards and her regrets. Unfortunately, on the last trip into town she picked up a bug. Now, I'm happy to say that's not a situation for me, like the two sons of Ireland who were in the pub one evening and one asked the other about his wife. And he said, 'Oh, she's terribly sick.' He said, 'She's terribly ill.' And the other one says. 'Oh, I'm sorry to hear that.' But he said,' Is there any danger?' 'Oh,' he said, 'no. She's too weak to be dangerous anymore.'"

—*Remarks in New York City at the eighty-fourth annual dinner of the Irish American Historical Society; 11/6/81*

"Secretary of the Interior Jim Watt would have been here, but he's working on a lease 'for strip mining the Rose Garden."

—*Remarks on presenting a check for the Westway highway project to Mayor Edward Koch in New York City; 9/7/81*

"The other day, when all those ballplayers were out there on the South Lawn on that big baseball day that we had, Jim Watt told me out there that when he was a boy, he dreamed of one day being out in center field at Yankee Stadium—drilling oil."

—*Remarks at the annual awards dinner of the White House News Photographers' Association; 5/18/83*

Question: "What if he [Jim Watt] strikes oil in the corral [at your ranch]?"
The President: "I'll cut him in."
  —*Question-and-answer session with reporters at Rancho del Cielo, Calif.; 8/31/81*

"I've discovered how nice people can be. I got a letter from an environmentalist the other day, and he was thanking me. He said it's the first time he's ever been able to make his children behave. He now scares them into being good by telling 'em James Watt will get 'em."
  —*Remarks at a dinner marking the fortieth anniversary of United Service Organizations, Inc.; 10/17/81*

"And sometimes when a Cabinet meeting starts to drag, I wonder what would happen if the jellybean jar there at the Cabinet table was filled with jalapeno jellybeans."
  —*Remarks at the Annual Convention of the American G.I. Forum in El Paso, Tex.; 8/13/83*

"I even have some of them [Irishmen] in my Cabinet. One of them traces his maternal roots to Mithcellstown, just down the road from Ballyporeen. And he and I have almost the same name. I'm talking about Don Regan. He spells it R-e-g-a-n. We're all of the same clan, we're all cousins. I tried to tell the Secretary that his branch of the family spelled it that way because they just couldn't handle as many letters as ours could."
  —*Remarks to the citizens of Ballyporeen, Ireland; 6/3/84*

[After reports claimed that then Chief of Staff Donald Regan maintained near complete control of the White House staff]
"The other day when I told Don Regan I was opposed to dictators whoever or wherever they are, he asked me if he should start packing."
>—*Remarks at the annual White House Correspondents' Association dinner; 4/17/86*

"One of you just recently wrote a piece questioning why things seem to be going so well for me lately. Well, it's just a case of letting Reagan be Regan."
>—*Remarks at the annual White House Correspondents' Association dinner; 4/17/86*

[Amid reports that Nancy Reagan and then Chief-of-Staff Don Regan were feuding]
"Nancy and Don at one point tried to patch things up. They met privately over lunch. Just the two of them and their food tasters."
>—*Remarks at the annual White House Correspondents' Association dinner; 4/22/87*

"And now, I've been looking forward to cutting this ribbon. I've been practicing all morning on Ed Meese's tie."
>—*Remarks at the reopening of the press briefing room at the White House; 11/9/81*

"And by the way, why are you all so willing to carry the bad news about this administration? Now, you all did stories about the Vice President taking a dive at the bowling alley, but no one mentioned that he knocked down nine pins. And if he had slid just a little further, he'd have caught

the tenth with his head. 'Bowling for Dollars' wants him to
do a guest spot."
    *—Remarks at the annual White House Correspon-
    dents' Association dinner; 4/13/84*

[Referring to a personally offensive advertisement published in *Penthouse* magazine which prompted the Reverend Jerry Falwell to respond with a libel suit:]
"And while I have the opportunity with so many of the
press, I want you to know that it is not true that the Moral
Majority has been trying to exert undue influence. That
rumor started recently when Jerry Falwell called me with a
suggestion for ambassador to Iran: the publisher of *Penthouse.*"
    *—Remarks at the annual Salute to Congress dinner;
    2/4/81*

"It's been an exciting time, and I admit sometimes a pain-
ful and difficult one. This came home to me when I was
discussing our belt-tightening measures with President
Ford, while we were also talking about his new library and
museum in Michigan. I found myself feeling very envious
of him. So I came back, and with an eye on the future, I
spoke to Dave Stockman about that subject. He tells me
he's been pricing bookmobiles."
    *—Remarks and a question-and-answer session with a
    group of out-of-town editors; 10/5/81*

"It reminds me of a story that my friend Punch Sulzberger
tells about the time he had lunch at the White House. That
evening he went home and called his mother, who is the
most remarkable woman. And he said to her, 'Mother,
today I had lunch at the White House with the President of

the United States, the Vice President of the United States, and the Secretary of State.' 'Yes dear,' his mother said dryly, 'and what did they want?'"

—Remarks and a question-and-answer session with the American Society of Newspaper Editors; 4/9/86

"They tell me I'm the most powerful man in the world. I don't believe that. Over there in that White House someplace there's a fellow that put a piece of paper on my desk every day that tells me what I'm going to be doing every fifteen minutes. He's the most powerful man in the world."

—Remarks at a meeting with Asian and Pacific-American leaders; 2/23/84

The Reagan
Stand-up Routine

"[There was a] fellow that wanted a job at the zoo taking care of the animals. And he got the job. But then they told him the first thing he'd have to do was wear the gorilla suit and perform for the kids, because the gorilla had died. And he was a little upset, but they said, 'You'll only have to do that until the new gorilla gets here.' So he was in the cage, and finally, with all the kids out there looking at him, he got carried away. And he was swinging on a trapeze, and he swung himself clear over into the lions' cage. And a lion came roaring at him and jumped on him, and he went down screaming for help. And the lion said, 'Shut up, or you'll get us both fired.'"
—*Remarks in Denver, Colo.; 9/8/86*

"It was back in those vaudeville days. People trying out for vaudeville would come in, empty theater, out on the stage, down there in front would be sitting a very cynical agent with a cigar, usually in his mouth, and he'd say okay, and they'd do their stuff. Well, this particular day a young fellow came out on center stage, out came the cigar. He says, 'Okay, what do you do, kid?' and the young fellow took off and flew around the ceiling of the theater up over the balconies and everything, and came down to a perfect landing. And the agent said: 'Well, all right. What else do you do besides bird imitations.' "

—*Remarks in Washington, D.C.; 2/9/87*

"[There] is a story about an elderly couple who were getting ready for bed one night, and she said, 'Oh, I just am so hungry for ice cream, and there isn't any in the house.' And he said, 'I'll get some.' 'Oh,' she said, 'you're a dear.' And she said, 'Vanilla with chocolate sauce.' He says, 'I won't forget.' She said, 'With some whipped cream on top.' And he says, 'Vanilla with chocolate sauce, whipped cream on top.' And she said, 'And a cherry.' And he said, 'And a cherry on top.' Well, she said, 'Please write it down. I know you'll forget.' And he said, 'I won't forget. Vanilla with chocolate sauce, whipped cream, and a cherry on top.' And away he went. By the time he got back, she was already in bed, and he handed her the paper bag. She opened it and there was a ham sandwich. And she said, 'I told you to write it down. You forgot the mustard.' "

—*Remarks at a dinner honoring Senator Russell Long; 10/16/85*

"It's a little like that old story of the traveling salesman who was having kind of a rough day of it and finally gave up and dropped into a local diner and wearily ordered a cup of coffee and a couple of eggs and a few kind words. And the waitress brought the order, put down the eggs, and put down the coffee, and said, 'Will there be anything else?' Well, he said, 'What about the kind words?' She said, 'Don't eat them eggs.' "

—*Remarks in Richmond, Va.; 3/28/88*

"I do feel very much at home here in your lovely farm and dairy country. I'm a rancher myself. I take a little kidding now and then in Washington about our ranch. But you know, even some Midwesterners admit that cattle fit right into the California scene. They stand around all day in the sun, no clothes on, eating salad. I just want to assure you that the cows in California are the same as cows in Minnesota. Except, of course, in California, they have their teeth capped."

—Remarks in Minneapolis, Minn.; 6/9/83

"Well, it does remind me of a story, and I have to have something to start with. It was about a—it's a true story, I understand, about a newspaper photographer out in Los Angeles. He's called in by his editor and told of a fire that was raging out there in Palos Verdes. That's a hilly area south of Los Angeles, a lovely residential area. His assignment was to rush down to a small airport, board a waiting plane, get some pictures of the fire, and be back in time for the afternoon edition.

Well, he raced down the freeway. He broke the law all the way. He got to the airport and drove his car to the end of the runway. And sure enough, there was a plane waiting with all the engines all there revved up, ready to go. He got aboard, and at about five thousand feet, he began getting his camera out of the bag, told the fellow flying the plane to get him over the fire so he could get his pictures and get back to the paper. And from the other side of the cockpit there was a deafening silence. And then he heard these words: 'Aren't you the instructor?' "

—Remarks at the twenty-fifth anniversary of the National Aeronautics and Space Administration; 10/19/83

"A farmer once won a sweepstakes, thousands and thousands of dollars, and someone asked him what he planned to do with all the money. And he said, 'I'll just keep on farming till it's all gone.'"

—Remarks on National Agriculture Day; 3/21/83

"You know, there's a story about a young fellow from the city who hired out to work on a farm during the harvest season. And the first morning everyone was up well before dawn. The new hired hand and the farmer made their way in the dark out to the oat field and neither one of them saying a word. And finally the city fellow asked what kind of oats were they going to cut—wild oats or tame oats. The farmer, a little surprised, said, 'Well, tame oats, of course. Why do you ask?' 'Well,' he said, 'I was just wondering why we're sneaking up on 'em in the dark.'"

—Remarks at the annual meeting of the American Farm Bureau Federation in Dallas, Tex.; 1/11/83

"I was speaking to a farm group in Las Vegas. And on the way to where I was to speak, there was one of those fellows that was there for the action, and he recognized me. And he said, 'What are you doing here?' And I told him. He said, 'What are a bunch of farmers doing in Las Vegas?' And I just couldn't help it. I said, 'Buster, they're in a business that makes a Las Vegas crap table look like a guaranteed annual income.'"

—Remarks at a dinner honoring Secretary of Agriculture John Block; 3/17/81

"It was about a fellow that was driving down a country road, and there beside him was a chicken—he was doing about forty-five and the chicken was running alongside. So

he stepped on the gas, he got it up to about sixty, and the chicken caught up with him and was right beside him again, and then he thought as he was looking at him that the chicken had three legs. But before he could really make up his mind for sure, the chicken took off out in front of him at sixty miles an hour and turned down a lane into a barnyard. Well, he made a quick turn and went down into the barnyard, too, and there was a farmer standing there, and he asked him, he said, 'Did a chicken come past you?' And he said, 'Yeah.' 'Well,' he said, 'am I crazy or did the chicken have three legs?' He says, 'Yep, it's mine.' He says, 'I breed three-legged chickens.' And the fellow said, 'For heaven sakes, why?' Well, he says, 'I like the drumstick, and Ma likes the drumstick, and now the kid likes drumsticks and we just got tired of fighting for it.' And the driver said, 'Well, how does it taste?' He says, 'I don't know. I've never been able to catch one.'"
  —*Remarks at a fund-raising dinner for Senator Mack Mattingly of Georgia; 6/5/85*

". . . like the story of the three fellows who went into a restaurant. They were ordering their dinner, and one of them ordered a glass of milk. But he told the waitress that he'd been in there the week before, ordered a glass of milk, and he wanted a clean glass this time. Well, the other two also decided to order milk. When the waitress came back with the three glasses of milk, she said, 'Now, which of you wanted the clean glass?'"
  —*Remarks in Columbia, Mo.; 5/26/87*

"Last month, in California, when people applauded, I didn't know if they were clapping or swatting Medflies."
  —*Remarks in Denver, Colo.; 9/18/81*

"I wonder how many of you know about the Quaker whose patience was sorely tried when the cow he was trying to milk kept kicking the milk pail over. Finally, he got up from the milking stool, faced the cow, and said, 'Thou knowest I cannot strike thee. Thou knowest I cannot even curse thee. But dost thou knowest I can sell thee to someone who will?' "

—Radio address to the nation; 6/1/85

"Seems that a farmer from New Hampshire was visiting a rancher in Texas. And he was driving down the highway, and there was a Texan driving on the highway. And there was an accident, and they collided. Well, they got talking then a little bit, and the Texan took the—no real damage to the cars—and the Texas took the New Hampshirite out and said if he needed a lift he'd give him a lift. He said, 'Well, let me show you our place down here.' So, they got in the car, and he started. And he drove him past some longhorn cattle, and then he showed him how high the corn grew and finally ended up bragging about the size of the ranch itself. He said, 'Just imagine, you know,' he says, 'I can start in the morning and drive all day—one side of my ranch—and I never get to the other side.' The New Hampshirite says, 'Yup. I got an old pickup truck just like that.' "

—Remarks at a dinner for members of the Republican Governors Association; 10/7/86

"[There's a] story about the old farmer who took over a parcel of land down near the creek bottom. It had never been cleared, it was covered with rocks, brush, all rutted, and he just determined to make it flourish. And he went to

work and he hauled away the rocks and fertilized and so
forth, and then planted his garden and before long just had
a very beautiful garden.

And he was so proud of what he'd accomplished that
one Sunday after church he asked the minister to drop by
and see his place. Well, the reverend came out and he was
impressed. He said, 'That's the tallest corn I've ever seen.
The Lord certainly has blessed this land.' And then he
said, 'Those melons! I've never seen any bigger than that.
Praise the Lord.' And he went on that way—tomatoes,
squash, the beans, everything, and what the Lord had
done with that land. And the old farmer was getting pretty
edgy. And finally he couldn't take it anymore and he said,
'Reverend, I wish you could have seen it when the Lord
was doing it by Himself.' "

—Remarks in Chicago, Ill.; 1/31/84

"You know, apparently the town rogue of one small Irish
hamlet lay on his deathbed as the priest prepared for the
atonement. 'Do you renounce the devil? Do you renounce
him and all his works?' the priest asked. And the rogue
opened one eye and said, 'Father, this is no time for making enemies.' "

*—Remarks at Notre Dame University, South Bend,
    Ind.; 3/9/88*

"I remember when Ezra Taft Benson was Secretary of
Agriculture. And he was out in the country and hearing
reports from people in the farm areas and talking to them,
and at one place there was a fellow that was giving him a
really bad time, really complaining. And Ezra turned
around and looked at some notes that someone handed
him and then turned back and said, 'Now, wait a minute.'

He said, 'You didn't have it so bad.' He said, 'You had twenty-six inches of rain this last year.' And the fellow said, 'Yes, I remember the night it happened.'"
    —*Remarks at a dinner honoring Secretary of Agriculture John Block; 3/17/81*

"I feel a little bit like the old farm gentleman who was in the bar one day, and two gentlemen with much more knowledge and sophistication than he had were discussing nuclear energy. And finally, aware of his presence and thinking they'd have a little joke, one of them said to the old farmer, 'Where would you like to be in the event of a nuclear explosion?' And the old boy said, 'Someplace where I could say, 'What was that?'"
    —*Remarks at the presentation ceremony for the Enrico Fermi awards at the Department of Energy; 4/25/83*

"A saying in colonial times suggested there are two ways to get to the top of an oak tree, where the view is much better. One is to climb; the other is to find an acorn and sit on it."
    —*Remarks at the Independence Day celebration; 7/3/87*

"[There was a] cub reporter whose first solo assignment was to interview a fellow who was just going to have a birthday that made him the oldest person in town. And he got to the address—it was an older building out on the outskirts of the city. An elderly gentleman ushered him in. And he sat down, and the reporter determined he was the man. And he said he was there for the interview, and he led right to the matter about how old are you, and the man said, 'Ninety-six.' He said, 'To what do you attribute your longevity?' And the fellow said, 'I don't smoke, drink, or run around with wild women.' And at that moment there was a crash from upstairs. And the reporter looked up and said, 'What was that?' And the old boy said, 'Oh, that's Dad, he's drunk again.'"

—*Remarks at a White House briefing on tax reform; 6/10/86*

"This joke was told to me by a minister—Bill Alexander—who used to do the invocation for the Republican conventions. And he heard me speak once. And after he'd heard me speak, he told me about his first experience as a preacher. And I've always thought there was a connection.

He said that he had worked for weeks on that first sermon. He'd been invited to preach at a little country church out in Oklahoma, and he went there well prepared, and stood up in the pulpit for an evening service, and looked out at one lone little fellow sitting out there among all the empty pews. So he went down, and he said, 'My friend, you seem to be the only member of the congregation that showed up, and I'm just a young preacher getting started. What do you think? Should I go through with it?' And the fellow says, 'Well, I don't know about that sort of thing, I'm a little old cowpoke out here in Oklahoma. But I do know this—if I loaded up a truckload of hay, took it out in the prairie, and only one cow showed up, I'd feed her.'

Well, Bill took that as a cue. And he said—an hour and a half later, he said, 'Amen.' And he went down, and he said, 'My friend, you seem to have stuck with me. I'm just a young preacher getting started. What do you think?'

'Well,' he says, 'like I told you, I don't know about

that sort of thing, but I do know this—if I loaded up a truckload of hay and took it out in the prairie and only one cow showed up, I sure as hell wouldn't give her the whole load.' "

—*Remarks at the Executive Exchange Commission;*
   10/6/86

"[There is] a story of an old preacher who was talking to a young preacher who hadn't had as much experience. And he said to him, 'You know, sometimes on Sunday morning, they begin to nod off.' And he says, 'I've found a way to wake them up.' He says, 'Right in my sermon when I see them beginning to doze, I say, "Last night I held in my arms a woman who is the wife of another man." And he says, 'That wakes them up.' And he says, 'Then, when they look at me startled, I say: It was my dear mother.'

Well, the young preacher took that to heart. And a few weeks later, sure enough, there some of them were, dozing off. So, he remembered what had been told to him, and he said, 'Last night I held in my arms a woman who is the wife of another man.' And they all looked at him, and everyone was awake. And he says, 'I can't remember who it was.' "

—*Remarks at the Southern Republican Leadership*
   Conference in Atlanta, Ga.; 1/26/84

"There was a minister who put his text on the pulpit a half an hour before every service. And one Sunday a smart aleck hid the last page. And the minister preached powerfully, but when he got to the words, 'So Adam said to Eve,' he was horrified to discover that the final sheet was gone. And riffling through the other pages, he stalled for time

repeating, 'So Adam said to Eve—'and then in a low voice said, 'There seems to be a missing leaf.' "
   —*Remarks at the Annual Convention of the National Association of Evangelicals in Columbus, Ohio; 3/6/84*

"Well, you remember Teddy [Roosevelt]—strong-willed, persuasive, and nothing could stop him. There used to be a story about him, that after he died, he got to heaven. And on his first day in heaven, he told Saint Peter, 'Your choir is weak, inexcusably weak. You should reorganize it at once.' And Saint Peter said, 'All right,' and gave T.R. the job. 'Well,' Teddy said, 'I'll need ten thousand sopranos, ten thousand altos, and ten thousand tenors.' 'But what about the basses?' asked Saint Peter. Teddy said, 'Don't worry about that. I'll sing bass.' "
   —*Remarks in Washington, D.C.; 3/30/88*

"You know, there's a story about a small-town charity. A new chairman was elected, and he was going through all the records as it came time for the annual charity drive, and he saw where one of the richest men in town had never given a penny. So he went to see him, and he said that he'd been going through the records, and he said, 'The records show that you have never given to the annual town charity.' And the man said, 'Well, do the records also show that I had a brother who was permanently injured as a result of a wound in World War II and is unable to work to take care of himself? Do they show that my sister was widowed with seven children left and no insurance and no means of support?' Well, the chairman, a little abashed, said, 'Well, no, our records don't show that.' 'Well,' he said, 'I don't give them anything. Why should I give something to you.?' "

—Remarks at the President's Volunteer Action awards luncheon; 6/30/87

"You know, on the way over, I remembered something that happened a long time ago when teachers could talk about things like religion in the classroom. And a very lovely teacher was talking to her class of young boys, and she asked, 'How many of you would like to go to heaven?' And all the hands instantly shot into the air at once, except one, and she was astounded. And she said, 'Charlie, you mean you don't want to go to heaven?' He said, 'Sure, I want to go to heaven, but not with that bunch.' "

—Remarks at the annual National Prayer Breakfast; 2/3/83

"It seems that a certain little boy had reached school age, and his mother worked very hard to make him enthusiastic about the idea—bought him new clothes, told him about the other children he would meet, got him so excited about the project that he eagerly went off on the first day, came home with excellent reports of what school was like. Well, the next morning, his mother went into the bedroom and said he had to get up, and he said, 'What for?' She said, 'You've got to go to school.' He said, 'What, again?' "

—Remarks at Suitland High School, Suitland, Md.; 1/20/88

"There's a story about a boy whose math homework paper was less than inspiring. When the boy's paper was handed back, the teacher said, 'I never saw so many errors in my

life. I just can't understand how one person could have made all these mistakes.' And the boy said, 'One person didn't; my father helped.'"
—*Remarks during a visit to Walt Disney World's EPCOT Center near Orlando, Fla.; 3/8/83*

[To a luncheon of teachers]
"But, you know, I've given toasts to kings and queens in this room, as well as to prime ministers and presidents, but you're the only group for whom I've ever felt obliged to diagram my sentences."
—*7/13/83*

[To another group of teachers]
"Well, it's wonderful to have all of you here today at the White House. We want you to enjoy our little get-together today. So please lean back, relax, and stop worrying about what the students are doing to the substitute teachers back home."
—*10/19/83*

"[There] was a teacher that was trying to impress her students, the children—winter had come along and the cold season and all. And she was trying to tell them how to avoid catching colds. And so she told a very heartrending tale which she said was about her one-time brother. And she said that she had this little brother and that he was a fun-loving little boy, and he went out with his sled. And he stayed out too long, and he caught cold. And when she'd finished with the tale, the way she told it, there was just dead silence in the room. And she thought she had really gotten to them. And then a voice in the back said, 'Where's his sled?' "

—*Remarks at A White House reception for the National Association of Elementary School Principals and the National Association of Secondary School Principals; 7/29/83*

"[A young teacher] was having trouble way down in the elementary grade in the patriotic ceremonies and saluting the flag, about explaining exactly where to put their right hand. And then modern style came to the rescue. He just told them put it on the alligator."

—*Remarks at a dinner in Long Beach, Calif.; 6/30/83*

"A few years ago, in the rebellious sixties and early seventies, we did see such a discarding of basic truths. It was a time when at least part of the generation of our sons and daughters declared that no one over thirty could be trusted. One wonders what they think now that they themselves have passed that thirty-year mark.

In those troubled times when no one was boasting about only living a stone's throw from the campus, I, as governor, couldn't go on our campuses in California without causing a demonstration. And then one day the student body presidents of our nine university campuses and some of their other student officers asked to have a meeting with me. Well, I was delighted. I said yes, because I was anxious to establish some kind of communication. They arrived, some of them barefoot, all of them were in T-shirts and jeans. And when we were all seated—maybe I should say slouched—their spokesman opened the meeting.

'Governor,' he said, 'it's impossible for you to understand us, to understand our generation.' Well, I tried to establish some base for conversation, and I said, 'Well, we know more about being young than you do about being old.' And he said, 'No, I'm serious. You can't understand your own sons and daughters. You didn't grow up in a world of instant electronic communications, of cybernetics, of men computing in seconds what it once took months and even years, of jet travel, nuclear power, and journeys into space and the moon.'

Well, you know, usually in a situation of that kind you don't think of the right answer until the meeting's over and you're at home, and then it's too late. But he went on in that vein just long enough for the Lord to provide the right words. And when he finished I said, 'You're absolutely right. We didn't have those things when we were growing up. We invented them.'"

—*Remarks at the 1981 White House Conference on Aging; 12/1/81*

[Toast to Chancellor Helmut Schmidt of West Germany]
"We've discussed significant issues that affect us—our NATO and security commitments, our economy and foreign policy, our desire for greater stability in the world. I must tell everyone here tonight, though, that one important matter was left off our agenda. I had hoped that we could resolve once and for all the relative advantages of Rhine wines versus California wines."

—*5/21/81*

"[There was this] fellow who went to the hospital for a complete checkup, very depressed, and said to the doctor, 'I look in the mirror, I'm a mess. My jowls are sagging. I have blotches all over my face. My hair has fallen out. I feel ugly. What is it?' And the doctor said, 'I don't know what it is, but your eyesight is perfect.' "

—*Remarks at the annual meeting of the American Medical Association House of Delegates in Chicago, Ill.; 6/23/83*

". . . I try to remember the case of the gentleman who went in for a physical examination and then said to the doctor, 'Okay. Give it to me straight. I can take it.' And the doctor said, 'Let me put it to you this way. Eat the best part of the chicken first.' "

—*Remarks announcing federal support of the National Health Fair Partnership Program; 8/5/82*

"While the quality of health care in this nation is unsurpassed, unfortunately, so are the costs. In fact many patients believe that a hospital should have the recovery room adjoining the cashier's office."

—*Remarks at the annual meeting of the American Medical Association House of Delegates in Chicago, Ill.; 6/23/83*

"I can't resist telling a little story here that also has to do with some gentlemen who—three of them arrived at the Pearly Gates together and were informed that there was only room for one. And they had decided inside that the man who participated in the oldest trade or profession would be the one that was allowed to come in. And the gentleman stepped forward and said, 'We know that the Lord made Adam and then created Eve out of a rib from Adam, and that took surgery. And I'm a surgeon, so I guess it's me.' But before he could move in, the second one said, 'Wait.' He said, 'Before the Lord did that he worked six days. Everything was chaos and he worked six days and created the earth. So,' he said, 'that makes Him an engineer, and I guess that calls for me.' And the third one stepped up and said, 'I'm an economist. Where do you think they got all that chaos?'"

> —*Remarks at a luncheon meeting for the United States Olympic Committee in Los Angeles, Calif.; 3/3/83*

"You know, it's said that an economist is the only professional who sees something working in practice and then seriously wonders if it works in theory."

> —*Remarks at the International Monetary Fund; 9/29/87*

"It seems an economist, a chemist, and an engineer were stranded on a desert island. And between them they had only a single can of beans, but no can opener. The engineer suggested that he climb a palm tree to a precise height, then throw the beans at a precise distance, at a precise angle. 'And when the can hits,' he said, 'it will split open.' 'No,' said the chemist. 'We'll leave the can in the sun until the heat causes the beans to expand so much the can will explode.' 'Nonsense, said the economist. 'Using either method we'd lose too many beans. According to my plan, there will be no mess or fuss and not a single bean will be lost.' The engineer and the chemist said, 'Well, we're certainly willing to consider it. What's your plan?' And the economist answered, 'Well, first assume we have a can opener.'"

> —*Remarks in Los Angeles, Calif.; 4/10/87*

"I learned a lot at Eureka [College], and not just about economics, which was my major. I think the principal thing I learned about economics as a major was that if you could place all the economists end to end, they'd never reach a conclusion."

> —*Remarks at a scholarship fund-raising dinner, Eureka College in Eureka, Ill.; 9/23/86*

"You know, I've heard that there is a new version of Trivial Pursuit, that game; it's called the economists' edition. In this one there are one hundred questions, three thousand answers."

> —*Remarks at a fund-raising dinner for Senator Robert Kasten, Wis.; 10/15/85*

". . . a friend of mine was asked to a costume ball a short time ago. He slapped some egg on his face and went as a liberal economist."

> —*Remarks in Washington, D.C.; 2/11/88*

"I heard of a fellow who had been unemployed for a long time, and a few days ago he found a job at a china warehouse. He'd only worked there a couple days when he smashed a large oriental vase. The boss told him in no uncertain terms that the money would be deducted from his wages every week until the vase was paid for. And the fellow asked, 'How much did it cost?' He told him three hundred dollars. And the fellow cheered and said, 'At last, I've found steady work.'"

> —*Remarks at the annual meeting of the National Alliance of Business; 10/5/81*

"And there are still some diehards who refuse to acknowledge that the changes we've made have had anything to do with America's dramatic progress in these last few years. They sort of remind me of the fellow who was asked which was worse, ignorance or apathy, and he said, 'I don't know, and I don't care.'"

—Remarks at a fund-raising luncheon for Senator Slade Gorton of Washington State; 12/2/85

"Since coming to Washington I've found that statistics can be a little slippery. There's a story about a lemon-squeezing contest at a state fair. The first man got up, and he was strong. He picked up the lemon and squeezed and squeezed and got out eighty percent of the juice. The crowd applauded, and he pulled open his jacket, and on his shirt it read 'bodybuilders club.' The next man got up, and he looked even stronger. He squeezed and squeezed, and he got out ninety percent of the juice. The crowd cheered, and he pulled open his jacket and his shirt said 'Police Athletic League.' The final contestant got up. He was thin and scrawny and slouched and was a little weak-looking. He picked up the lemon and began to squeeze, and out came a hundred and fifty percent of the juice. He pulled open his jacket, and his shirt said, 'State Association of Statisticians.'"

—Remarks announcing the nomination of Ann D. McLaughlin to be Secretary of Labor; 11/3/87

"There's a little story about the great Supreme Court Justice Benjamin Cardozo that makes the point. Many years ago, when he was serving on the Court, he received a letter from a member of the public, and it read: 'Dear Judge Cardozo, I read in the newspaper that you are a liberal

judge. Will you send me ten dollars, as I'm really very hard up.' "
— *Remarks at a briefing on the nomination of Robert Bork; 9/30/87*

"This fellow was so successful [in business] that he was opening a branch office, and he decided to order a floral decoration for the occasion. When he got to [the] opening, he was shocked to see that the inscription on the flowers read, 'Rest in peace.' On his way home, he stopped at the flower shop to register a complaint. And the shop owner heard him out and then said, 'Well, take it easy. Things aren't that bad. Just remember that someplace today there's somebody opening something up, and it said, 'Good luck in your new location.' "
— *Remarks at the midyear meeting of the National Association of Realtors; 5/10/84*

[Remarks to employees at the Ivorydale Soap manufacturing plant]
"From the beginning, Procter and Gamble has been an important ally in our fight for tax reform. I was talking to one of your executive officers earlier, and he had kind of a funny way of talking, but I couldn't have agreed more with what he was saying. He said there's a rising Tide of good Cheer and Joy in the land. We see new Zest in the economy every day. And all we need now is a Bold new Dash to Safeguard the Gain we've made already."
— *10/3/85*

"This story is about a man who started his own business. He did well, and bought a summer home in the country. And because he was good-natured, all of his relatives and his relatives' relatives took this as an invitation to visit all summer, every summer. One day the man was sitting with a young third niece-in-law, twice removed, who'd ignored hint after hint that she'd overstayed her welcome. Finally he sighed and said, 'There's no chance, is there, that you'll ever come on another visit here again?' 'Why,' she said, 'Uncle, why shouldn't I come back?' Well, he said, 'Well, how can you come back if you never go away?'"

—*Remarks at the National Federation of Independent Business national conference; 6/23/87*

"You probably know the story about the young fellow that once asked a stranger if he was from Texas, and the kid's father kind of took him in hand and he said, 'Son, I want you always to remember one thing: If a man comes from Texas he'll tell you without being asked; and if he doesn't come from Texas, there's no need to embarrass him."

—*Speech in Irving, Tex.; 10/11/82*

"They sent a Texas Ranger to a town where there was a riot, and the mayor met him, and the mayor looked over his shoulder and said, 'Well, where are the rest?' And he says, 'Well, you've only got one riot.'"

—*Remarks at Elmendorf Air Force Base, Alaska, en route to Japan and the Republic of Korea; 11/8/83*

"You know, I've never understood what's so bad about being a cowboy. I'm proud of my spurs. I've often said there's nothing better for the inside of a man than the outside of a horse."

—*Remarks in North Platte, Nebr.; 8/13/87*

[To country music singer and bar-owner Mickey Gilley]
". . . I understand that a real tough young cowboy came in
one night and said to one of your waiters there, 'I want a
real rare steak.' In about three minutes, the waiter was
back with a platter and a steak on it, and the kid took one
look at it and says, 'Take it back.' And he said, 'You said
you wanted a real rare steak.' And the kid said, 'I've seen
cows hurt worse than this get up and walk away.' "
    —*Remarks at a congressional barbecue; 9/18/85*

"He [Calvin Coolidge] was once asked by reporters how
many fish were in one of his favorite angling places, the
River Brule. Coolidge said the waters were estimated to
carry forty-five thousand trout. And then he said, 'I haven't
caught them all yet, but I sure have intimidated them.' "
    —*Remarks at the fourth annual convention of Con-
    cerned Women for America; 9/25/87*

"One thing your state [Alaska] is known for is its outside
activities, of course, especially hunting and fishing. And
that reminds me of a story. It's a story about down there in
the other forty-eight, a young fellow that was making quite
a killing fishing and selling the fish to the local restaurant in
this small town. And the game warden began to get a little
suspicious about the catch that he was bringing in every
day. So knowing the sheriff was an uncle of this young
fellow, he asked him why he didn't go fishing with his
nephew and find out where he was catching and how he
was catching all those fish. So the sheriff asked, and the
nephew said, 'Sure.'
    Elmer and the sheriff rowed out into the middle of the
lake, and the sheriff started to get ready to put his line in.
And Elmer reached in the tackle box, came out with a

stick of dynamite, lit the fuse, threw it in, [there was an] explosion, and the fish came belly-up. And he started to gather them in, and the sheriff says, 'Elmer, you have just committed a felony.' Elmer reached into the tackle box, came up with another stick of dynamite, lit the fuse, handed it to the sheriff, and said, 'Did you come here to fish or talk?' "

—*Remarks at Elmendorf Air Force Base, Alaska;*
  11/8/83

[To members of the National Rifle Association]
"Not too long ago, I had a very memorable visit from your officials. They walked into the Oval Office with some members of the 'F' troop of the Texas army. Now, when I saw how those fellows were dressed, and what they were packing, I didn't know whether to stretch out my hand, or make a run for it through the Rose Garden."

—*In Phoenix, Ariz.; 5/6/83*

"I have a story—it's a true incident—that involves a fellow Californian, Danny Villaneuva, who used to placekick for the Rams and then later became a sports announcer. . . . Danny, as a sports announcer, was having dinner one night over at the home of a young ball player with the Dodgers. He and the ball player were talking sports, and the young wife was bustling about getting the dinner ready. And the baby started to cry, and she, over her shoulder, said to her husband, 'Change the baby.' And he being a young fellow and kind of inexperienced along about that line as a father—he was embarrassed in front of Danny—and he said, 'What do you mean, change the baby?' He says, 'That's not my line of work. I'm a ball player.' And she turned around, put her hands on her hips, and she communicated.

She said, 'Look, Buster, you lay the diaper out like a diamond, you put second base on home plate, put the baby's bottom on the pitcher's mound, hook up first and third, slide home underneath. And if it starts to rain, the game ain't called; you start all over again.' "

—Remarks at the annual convention of the National League of Cities in Los Angeles, Calif.; 11/29/82

"It sort of reminds me of a story. It was about a baseball rookie and his know-it-all manager. He had a lot of problems with him. But a crucial game in the pennant race, tied up in the bottom of the ninth, and this rookie was called on as a pinch hitter. And he went in and won the ball game with a booming home run over the right center field bleachers. As he rounded third and crossed home plate with a big grin on his face and his hand extended, the manager was waiting for him, and the manager ripped into him. He said, 'Your stance was all wrong. Your swing was awkward. You held your arms too high.' And when he paused for a breath, the kid said, 'Yeah, but how about that distance?' "

—Remarks to the world champion New York Mets; 11/12/86

[Remarks in Chicago, Ill.]
"Flying in on Air Force One, I thought I saw a new building on the Chicago skyline. And then, as we got closer, I discovered it was William 'The Refrigerator' Perry."

—8/12/86

[During a phone conversation with Tom Flores, coach of the Superbowl champion L.A. Raiders]
"I have already had a call from Moscow. They think that Marcus Allen is a new secret weapon and they insist that we dismantle it. Now, they've given me an idea about that team that I just saw there of yours. If you'd turn them over to us, we'd put them in silos and we wouldn't have to build the MX."
—1/22/84

"It reminds me a little bit of the story of the man who took his young son-in-law out and was going to introduce him to golf, and told him all that he had to do, and teed up the ball. And the kid took a swing, and he missed the golf ball entirely, but hit an ant's nest into the air. And so he lined up and took a crack at it and again—hit another gouge out of the ant's nest. And now there were ants flying all the way through the air. And as he lined up for the third try, two ants peeked out of the crater that he left, and one of them said, 'If we want to survive this, we'd better get on the ball.'"
—Remarks at a White House briefing; 6/6/86

"It seems that on a Sunday morning this man preferred to read the paper. And his son, little Billy, came at him with a glove and a ball and wanted him to come out in the yard and play ball. And he wanted to read the paper. And he noticed that on the front of the paper was a map of the world in connection with some story. And he hastily cut the map of the world out, cut it into pieces, and then said to Billy, 'Here, you take this and put the map of the world together, and when you get back, why, then, we'll go out and play ball.' He figured he'd have plenty of time to read

the paper. Billy was back in seven minutes. And he said,
'How did you do that so fast?' Well, he said, 'On the other
side of the map there was a picture of a family, and I found
that if you put the family together, then the world took care
of itself.' "

Remarks in West Lafayette, Ind.; 4/9/87

"I even offered to bring over some White House cuff links
as souvenirs for all of you, but I was told you prefer the
NSA [National Security Agency] cuff links—you can tune
in the Redskins game."

*—Remarks at dedication ceremonies for new facili-
ties, National Security Agency; 9/26/86*

"Actually, I was thinking on the way over that this is the
second gathering of attorneys I've addressed in the last
few months. When I spoke to the American Bar Association a short time ago, I said how disappointed I was that
the White House counsel wouldn't let me accept the honor-
arium. I was really looking forward to the first time I ever
talked to a group of lawyers and came home with the fee."

*—Remarks at a White House briefing of United States
Attorneys; 10/21/85*

"You know, there was a little tad that was in court in New
York, bandaged from his toe to his chin, suing for four
million dollars as the result of an accident, and he won the
suit. The lawyers for the insurance company went over to
him, and they said, 'You're never going to enjoy a penny of
this. We're going to follow you twenty-four hours a day. We
know you're faking, and the first time you move, we'll have
you.' He said, 'Will you now? Well,' he said, 'let me tell
you what's going to happen to me.' He said, 'They're

coming in here with a stretcher. We're flying direct to Paris, France, and there they're taking me on the stretcher off the plane, putting me in another ambulance. We're going direct to the shrine of Lourdes, and there you're going to see the damndest miracle you ever saw.'"
—Remarks at a reception for members of the Associated Contractors of America; 3/16/81

"You know, one of the pleasures that I get in visiting you is that I get to tell stories that folks up in Washington don't always understand. Stories, for example, that might involve a little Southern humor. For example, that incident where a Yankee from up North was down here driving on one of your highways and found himself in a collision with a car driven by one of the local citizens. They both get out of their cars, which were badly damaged, but neither one of them is hurt. And with true Southern hospitality, the Southerner said to the Yankee, 'You look a little upset. Wait just a minute.' And he reached into the back end of his car and came out with a bottle. He says, 'Here, take a shot of this. I think it will calm your nerves.' So he did and started to hand the bottle back. He says, 'No, no. Go ahead. You really are upset. This will help you. Take a couple of more drinks.' And he did. Finally, the Yankee said, 'Well, wait a minute. I'm drinking all this myself. Here, don't you want to drink it?' He says, 'No, I'll just stand here and wait until the police arrive.'"
—Remarks in Montgomery, Ala.; 9/18/86

"There was a fellow that was on his way to a mountain resort, and a policeman stopped him and said, 'Did you know you're driving without taillights?' And the driver hopped out of the car. He was so badly shaken that the officer took pity on him and said, 'Well, now, wait a minute. Calm down. It's not that serious an infraction.' The fellow said, 'It may not mean much to you, but to me it means I've lost my trailer, my wife, and four kids!' "

—Remarks at a meeting with senior presidential appointees; 9/8/87

". . . like the blacksmith on the Missouri jury. The judge asked him if he was prejudiced against the defendant, and he said, 'Oh, no, judge. We ought to give the bum a fair trial before we string him up.' "

—Remarks in Independence, Mo.; 9/2/85

"I've just spoken to a national meeting here in your city a few moments ago, the police chiefs of not only the nation but internationally—sheriffs—a tremendous crowd. I spoke to them about crime, and I'm happy to tell you that they're against it."

—Remarks in New Orleans, La.; 9/28/81

"I can't help but interject here about the fellow that knocked on another man's door, and when he came to the door, said, 'Do you own a black pit bull?' And the fellow said, 'Yes.' 'Well,' he said, 'I have to tell you it's dead.' He said, 'What do you mean it's dead? What happened?' And he says, 'My Pekinese killed it.' He says, 'Your Pekinese killed it? How?' He said, 'It got stuck in his throat.' "

—Remarks at the National Alliance of Business; 9/14/87

"Back in the thirties, when there was a citizen military training program, and then every summer they'd have a couple of weeks of camp and military maneuver or war game, and usually some brass from Washington would be invited to come out and lend prestige to it. And I was getting a commission in the cavalry reserve at Fort Des Moines at that time. Over at Fort Omaha was the summer affair and the battle and all, and we had horse cavalry then. And the commanding officer at Fort Omaha and the visiting general from Washington were standing there and someone sent a young reserve lieutenant, horse-mounted, over with a message. And he went over with a splash. He came in there full-speed, pulled up the horse. The horse must have had a sore mouth because he put on the brakes on all four feet, and he somersaulted right over the head of the horse—landed on his feet holding the reins and was facing the two generals. So he snapped a salute, and the general from Washington very slowly and deliberately, as he returned the salute, said to the commanding officer, 'Does he always dismount like that?' "

—*Remarks by the President to the American Legion Washington Leadership Conference; 2/10/87*

"It was during World War II, and British Field Marshal Montgomery had come to America to help spur the war effort. A dinner was held in his honor in Hollywood. Sam Goldwyn, one of the founders of MGM, was to toast Field Marshal Montgomery. And when the time came, Sam, who has a reputation for misspeaking, got up, waited for silence, then after a few words said, 'I propose a toast to Marshal Field Montgomery.' Well, Jack Warner was sitting next to Sam and tried to help. And he said, 'Montgomery Ward, you mean.' "

—*Remarks to the Veterans of Foreign Wars; 3/7/88*

"There's a story about John Paul Jones' chief gunner's mate. It was during the gore and thunder of that most historic battle. He was loading and firing cannon and carrying the wounded to the medical officer, cutting away the tangled rigging. And apparently in the midst of that first fight, John Paul Jones went below momentarily and changed into a new uniform. And as he emerged on the deck a voice rang out through the smoke and fire—it was the British captain asking, 'Have you struck your colors?' And the gunner's mate, sweat and blood dripping from his body, turned and saw Jones now in his fresh uniform reply: 'I have not yet begun to fight.' And the gunner's mate said, "There's always somebody who didn't get the word.'"

—Address at commencement exercises at the United States Naval Academy; 5/22/85

"It reminds me of a favorite little story of mine about a career naval officer who finally got his four stripes, became a captain, and then was given command of a giant battleship. And one night he was out steaming around the Atlantic when he was called from his quarters to the bridge and told about a signal light in the distance. And the captain told the signalman, 'Signal them to bear starboard.' And back came the signal from ahead asking—or saying, '*You* bear to starboard.' Well, as I say, the captain was very aware that he was commander of a battleship, the biggest thing afloat, the pride of the fleet; and he said, 'Signal that light again to bear to starboard now.' And once again, back came the answer, 'Bear to starboard yourself.' Well, the captain decided to give his unknown counterpart a lesson in seagoing humility; so he said, 'Signal them again and tell them to bear to starboard. I am a battleship.'

And back came the signal, 'Bear to starboard yourself. I'm a lighthouse.' "
                    —*Remarks in Washington; 1/30/86*

"It was General Douglas MacArthur and Admiral Chester Nimitz, and during one of the campaigns in the South Pacific, they were changing ships and the waves overturned the small boat they were in. And Admiral Nimitz called out to General MacArthur for help, and the general finally got to him and held him above water, so he could breathe, until they were finally rescued. And when it was all over, the admiral said, 'Doug,' he said, 'please don't ever tell my men I can't swim.' And Doug said, 'I won't tell them that you can't swim if you won't tell them I can't walk on water.' "
                    —*Remarks in York, Pa.; 5/6/87*

"You know, there was a fellow riding a motorcycle one cold winter day. The wind coming in through the buttons of his jacket were chilling him, and finally he stopped, turned the jacket around, put it on backwards, took off again. Well, that solved the wind problem, but he hit a patch of ice; his arms were kind of restricted; he skidded into a tree. And when the police got there and elbowed their way through the crowd that had gathered and they said, 'What happened?' They said, 'We don't know. When we got here, he seemed to be all right. But by the time we had his head turned around straight, he was dead.' "
                    —*Remarks at the centennial meeting of the Supreme Council of the Knights of Columbus in Hartford, Conn.; 8/3/82*

"Well, when you read how the Torres brothers chased down a purse-snatcher wielding a knife; how Mrs. Keneally, a grandmother, collared a pickpocket by his neck scarf and gave him the back of her hand until the police arrived—I liked the picture of that one more than anything—and how Rabbi Rosenfeld immobilized a mugger armed with a machete, you realize there's nothing very average about the average American."

—*Remarks to* The Daily News *Crime Fighter award winners in New York City; 4/27/83*

"I remember a story about Lyndon Johnson when he was President. He was leaving the South Lawn of the White House, and the two helicopters were there, and he happened to be going toward the wrong one. And one of the security [guards] stepped up and didn't want to, with all the press covering this, make it obvious, said, 'Mr. President, that's your helicopter over there.' And Lyndon stopped and said, 'Son, they're all mine.'"

—*Remarks in Houston, Tex.; 11/13/81*

[Remarks commemorating the centennial of Harry Truman's birth]
"By 1948 the joke of the day was, 'To err is Truman.' Tom Dewey was picking his Cabinet. At the Democratic convention they carried signs that said, 'We're just mild about Harry.' Even the symbolism was against him. When he walked into the convention hall, they released fifty doves that had been hidden under a liberty bell as a symbol of peace. The doves were weak from the heat and the long confinement. The first one fell dead on the floor. Another circled frantically looking for a landing place, a safe

place—finally spotted a smooth and shiny perch, and it was Sam Rayburn's head."
—*5/8/84*

"Winston Churchill was once asked, 'Doesn't it thrill you, Mr. Churchill, to know that every time you make a speech, the hall is packed to overflowing?' 'It's quite flattering,' Winston replied, 'but whenever I feel this way, I always remember that if instead of making a political speech I was being hanged, the crowd would be twice as big.'"
—*Remarks in Washington, D.C.; 4/29/87*

". . . . like the time that the late Marilyn Monroe met Albert Einstein. Marilyn grabbed him by the arm and said, 'Let's get married.' Einstein looked at her and said, 'My dear, what if our children had my looks and your brains?'"
—*Remarks at a Republican Senate/House fund-raising dinner; 5/21/86*

"We had an actor that was in Hollywood, and he was only there long enough to get enough money to go to Italy, because he aspired to an operatic career. And then after some time there, in Milan, Italy, where he was studying, he was invited to sing at La Scala, the very spiritual fountainhead of the opera. They were doing 'Pagliacci,' and he sang the beautiful aria 'Vesti la giubba.' And he received such thunderous and sustained applause from the balconies and the orchestra seats that he had to repeat the aria as an encore. And again, the same sustained, thunderous applause, and again he sang 'Vesti la giubba.' And this went on until finally he motioned for quiet, and he tried to tell them how full his heart was at that reception—his first time out. But he said, 'I have sung "Vesti la

giubba" nine times now. My voice is gone. I cannot do it
again.' And a voice from the balcony said, 'You'll do it till
you get it right.' "
 —Remarks in Washington, D.C.; 2/11/88

"You know, Mark Twain once remarked that he spent
twenty-five dollars to research his family tree, and then he
had to spend fifty to cover it up."
 —Remarks in Seattle, Wash.; 8/23/83

[Greeting the finalists of the National Spelling Bee]
"Mark Twain was on a ship going across Europe. And in
the dining salon that night at dinner, someone wanting to
impress him at the table asked him to pass the sugar and
then said, 'Mr. Twain, don't you think it's unusual that
sugar is the only word in our language in which *s-u* has the
shu sound?' And Mark Twain said: 'Are you sure?' "
 —6/6/83

"This is a long way from the days of Ginger Rogers. Ginger
Rogers' partner, Fred Astaire—he was getting all of the
credit. And suddenly he began to realize Ginger was doing
the same thing on high heels and backwards."
 —Remarks in Baltimore, Md.; 10/15/86

"It goes without saying that I'm delighted to be here on
this very special day for the Irish and all who wish they
were Irish."
 —Toasts at a St. Patrick's Day luncheon hosted by the
  Irish ambassador; 3/17/81

[To representatives of the Hispanic community]
"I could confess something, and my people of my own
background wouldn't hold it against me: I think that if the
country were just left to us Anglos, it would be kind of
dull."

—9/16/81

"It has to do with a young fellow that arrived in New York
Harbor from Ireland, an immigrant to our country. And a
short time later, he started across one of those busy New
York streets against the light. And one of New York's
finest, a big policeman, grabbed him and said, 'Where did
you think you're going?' 'Well,' he says, 'I'm only trying to
get to the other side of the street there.' Well, when that
New York policeman, Irish himself, heard that brogue,
'Well,' he said, 'now, lad, wait.' He says, 'You stay here
until the light turns green, and then you go to the other side
of the street.' 'Aah,' he says, 'the light turns green.' Well,
the light turned orange for just a few seconds, as it does,
and then turned green, and he started out across the street.
He got about fiften feet out and he turned around, and he
says, 'They don't give them Protestants much time, do
they?'"

   —*Remarks at the annual convention of the Knights of
      Columbus, Chicago, Ill.; 8/5/86*

[During a meeting with Puerto Rican leaders]
"Success will not come easy, but it will come. And to
make it happen, America needs the help of all Americans,
including those from *la isla de encanto.* You'll forgive me
for stumbling on that one word there. It's so close to St.
Patrick's Day, I've been rehearsing me Irish."

   —3/15/84

"And, Mr. Foreign Minister, Mr. Ambassador, those of Irish heritage and those not so fortunate, would you join me in a toast to the President and the people of Ireland."

—Remarks on St. Patrick's Day at the Irish embassy; 3/17/83

"So, when I think of Italian families, I never think of loneliness but of warm kitchens and even warmer love. I heard a story the other day about a family that lived in a little apartment, but decided to move to a big house in the country. And a friend said to the twelve-year-old-son, Tony, 'How do you like your new house?' And he said, 'We love it. I have my own room. My brother has his own room. My sisters have their own rooms. But poor Mom, she's still in with Dad.' "

—Remarks at the San Gennaro Festival in Flemington, N.J.; 9/17/82

"And may I conclude with a little Irish blessing—although some suggest it's a curse: may those who love us, love us. And those who don't love us, may God turn their hearts. And if He doesn't turn their hearts, may He turn their ankles so we'll know them by their limping."

—Remarks at a meeting with senior presidential appointees; 9/8/87